The Doctor Who Dared to be Different

To our dear friend, Connie Wahlin
   you are such an inspiration
to so many.
   Love & hugs!
      Helen Warner
      5/2/03

ALL TRUTH PASSES THROUGH THREE STAGES:

FIRST, IT IS RIDICULED;

SECOND, IT IS VIOLENTLY OPPOSED;

AND FINALLY, IT IS ACCEPTED AS BEING SELF-EVIDENT

Schopenhauer

The Doctor Who Dared to be Different

His life, philosophy, diagnosis and treatment,

GLENN WARNER, M.D.

Lois Berry

Writers Club Press
San Jose New York Lincoln Shanghai

The Doctor Who Dared to be Different
His life, philosophy, diagnosis and treatment,
GLENN WARNER, M.D.

Writers Club Press
an imprint of iUniverse.com, Inc.

For information address:
iUniverse.com, Inc.
5220 S 16th, Ste. 200
Lincoln, NE 68512
www.iuniverse.com

ISBN: 0-595-18928-8

Printed in the United States of America

This book is dedicated to the memory of Glenn Warner on behalf of the thousands who loved him and survived cancer because of his knowledge and skills. And to his wife, Helen, who stood beside him for almost 56 years with her devotion and encouragement in every aspect of his career.

CONTENTS

ACKNOWLEDGEMENTS

I am deeply indebted to so many for their encouragement, expertise and helpful suggestions that made this book about a remarkable man possible. I give special recognition to the following:

To my sister, Ruth Bennett, for the many hours she spent editing and proofreading this book.

To Richard Stannard who read and critiqued parts of this book and conducted interviews with Glenn Warner.

To my son, Jim, and daughter, Barb, who have spent many hours instructing me on the computer. Just when I think I've learned it all, I get stuck again.

For the constant loving support of my daughter-in-law, Chris, daughters Jody and Ruth. To my awesome grandchildren Kelly, Jaime, Ronee, Mark, Jenn and Jeff.

Gratitude for the hours of time Glenn Warner gave to share his philosophy and knowledge.

Finally, to all the wonderful people who have given me so much love and support and made my life such a joy.

INTRODUCTION

This book is devoted to acquainting you with a remarkable oncologist, Dr. Glenn Warner, who died November 11, 2000. He was different from his peers in the medical community because he did not accept the status quo. Early in his career, he became discouraged by the lack of success in treating his cancer patients with surgery, radiation and chemotherapy. This began a life-long search for better and more humane therapies. He dared to use treatments deemed unacceptable by the medical community. The fact that these treatments included non-toxic drugs with minimal side effects was of little concern to a medical community threatened by his success.

The hundreds of long-time survivors in his care are testimonials to his approach. Many lives could have been saved if other oncologists had been willing to learn from this man.

People are thirsting for information regarding the best therapeutic regimen for themselves. They are seeking guidance from knowledge-able professionals of all types and especially those who will let the patients have some impute into their care. The greatest need for cancer patients today is to know the entire story about their illness and the possibilities for treatment.

Fear, anxiety and rage, the near-universal reactions to a diagnosis of cancer, need to be replaced with hope and confidence. The patient needs to have the assurance that his wishes will be considered in the choices made. A special support team needs to be formed around the patient to develop a positive attitude toward the treatment selected, which is then translated into probabilities rather than possibilities.

To be optimistic, a person needs to know the stories of recovery and to associate with long-term survivors. Support groups are filled with people who have survived for many years after being told there was nothing more that can be done for them. Our beliefs need to be consistent with current information, information that is the result of studies documenting the various treatment programs available. Attitudinal adjustments by family and friends are essential. This illness may have a focal point in one person, but it is truly a family affair.

The word *cancer* is neither a definite diagnosis nor a sentence. It merely reflects the symptom complex that is present at the moment in an ongoing process of carcinogenesis (cancer production). Dr. Lawrence LaShan wrote an excellent book depicting cancer as a turning point and certainly this is reflected in the attitude of people who are long-term survivors. Perhaps one of the failures of conventional oncologists today is their reluctance to learn from history and utilize the information that capable practitioners learned the hard way in handling these difficult problems

*   *   *   *

In 40 years as an oncologist, Dr. Warner said he witnessed patients survive all types of illnesses, regardless of the stage, and with a wide variety of doctors and treatment regimens. Skeptics say these are only anecdotal or spontaneous remissions, cannot be properly evaluated and should be disregarded. However, Warner believed there are no spontaneous remissions: that this is the way the body is supposed to work if allowed to do what it was designed to do.

Over the past several years, I was privileged to have many interviews with Dr. Warner about his education and training, philosophy, treatment for specific types of cancer, and his persecution by some in the medical community who had no substantial knowledge of the kind of care he administered to his patients. He was unique amongst doctors and men. I have never known a more caring, gentle, loving human being.

*   *   *   *

I could not say it better than John Robbins did in his book "Reclaiming Your Health." He said, "Glenn Warner reminds me of people like Semmelweis and Pasteur, physicians who saw a light their contemporaries did not, who suffered the scorn and condemnation of their colleagues, and who yet persevered to give something to humanity of immense and sustaining significance. He reminds me, as well, of Linus Pauling, who like Warner was both an eminent scientist and a distinguished humanitarian. And he brings to mind people like Mildred Nelson and Nurse Caisse, humble people who have asked nothing for themselves but the opportunity to be of service to their fellow human beings.

"Once when I was a child, a shiver went through me when I heard a man say that doctors were God's hands on earth.

He must have been thinking of doctors like Glenn Warner."

*   *   *   *

I have divided this book into four parts. Part I includes chapters on Warner's early years and education, his years at the Tumor Institute of Swedish Hospital Medical Center, Seattle, Washington, and study and research with immunologists Karl Erik and Ingegerd Hellstrom. I conclude this section with what I learned from the Food & Drug Administration (FDA) about the ongoing investigation at the Tumor Institute.

Part II takes the reader through the relentless persecution of this man by the Medical Quality Assurance Commission (MQAC). When you know the facts, I am sure you will believe, as I do, that because of the actions of a few hundreds of patients were denied their treatment of choice. The MQAC would have us believe that patients are not intelligent enough to decide what treatment for their cancer promised the most hope for their recovery.

Part III contains Warner's philosophy and a series of discussions on specific types of cancer in an effort to educate the reader as to the successful approach he used in his programs to fit the needs of each individual patient. Hopefully, this information will provide some insight into a type of complementary treatment that incorporated the best in conventional therapies with other modalities.

Part IV contains a chapter on the immune system and how it works. Also, what I learned from the FDA on the use of BCG and other biologic response modifiers. I close with a discussion of the history of cancer treatment and research. It is shocking how little progress has been made. This in spite of the billions of dollars spent in research.

PART I

WHO IS THIS MAN?

HOW DID HE BECOME A PIONEER IN THE TREATMENT OF CANCER? WHAT HAPPENED AT THE TUMOR INSTITUTE

CHAPTER 1

EARLY YEARS AND EDUCATION

Let us examine Warner's early years and education in an effort to understand what shaped him and inspired him. What was his background and what factors brought him into the medical profession and eventually into a different approach to the treatment of cancer? Certainly, he would have been better off professionally if he had stayed with the mainstream beliefs of his colleagues. His motivation was his patients and whatever methods would contribute to their health and well being.

Glenn Warner was born July 11, 1919, in Orting, Washington to Joseph and Edna Warner. His family was in the logging business in a very small town in Western Washington. His father was a two-fisted, hard-working man who ran a small logging operation. There was nothing about Joseph to indicate he would ever feel a need to go into something intellectually different. He had graduated from high school and then played semi-pro basketball before he went into the logging business near Shelton, Washington because it was the primary occupation in that small community.

His was a religious family who attended church regularly. When its minister collapsed and died, Joseph Warner was asked to assume the minister's duties. He realized that this was not possible with no training, but it ignited a desire in him that took his life in a new direction. He moved the family from Orting to various places where he could go to college and eventually theology school. Over the next six years, Joseph pursued his education and preached on the side in order to keep the family going. He received college degrees from the University of Oregon, the Eugene Bible University and a Baptist Theology School in Portland, Oregon. Getting an education became almost an obsession. He was successful in this new endeavor and rapidly advanced in his profession. Warner's mother, Edna, was always encouraging and willingly put up with the hardships that were necessary for him to accomplish his goals.

Joseph was an unpolished sort of person and his education didn't change that. However, his character, ethical behavior, and sense of fair play were qualities admired by his son as his father questioned everything and always stood up for what he thought was right.

Because of his integrity, he became influential with many people and when a seat in the State House of Representatives became available, friends persuaded him to run. 'Scoop' Jackson narrowly beat him, but they became friends and remained good friends the rest of their lives. Politics was not his calling; the ministry was.

Joseph then became involved with larger groups that were socially oriented, such as the Institution for Christian and Jews. He was the district leader of that group for a long time when anti-Semitism was rampant in this country. He fought discrimination and became a chaplain in prisons working for the rehabilitation of the inmates in addition to preaching in church. He lived into his early nineties.

*   *   *   *

Many examples of his father's life influenced Warner's later thinking. Their home was always open to everyone regardless of religious persuasion or race. He grew up in a home with four other siblings without many material things. His father was strict but loving and had high expectations for his children that he believed could only be attained through education.

When asked when he decided on medicine, Warner tells the story of a visitor to the family home, "One of the persons who came to our house a great deal was a general practitioner, Dr. Barendrick, from McMinnville, Oregon. I don't know why he made such an impression on me because he was called away so many times. The phone was ringing constantly for him. He would sit down to dinner, then leave and come back just as we were finishing. And, yet, for some reason I was impressed with what he was doing. I think it was because he was available to help others no matter where or what he was doing. Thinking back, as the years of college and medical school went on and on, I wondered if it was such a good idea for me because the cost was so great and my family had no money to help me. It was a struggle!"

World War II interrupted Warner's education as it did so many young men's in the 1940s. He was in his last year of school at Central Washington College and was taking pre-med courses when he learned there was a V12S program for individuals who would be drafted but had attained a certain degree of education and were interested in medicine. The government anticipated a long conflict and wanted to train more doctors. The V12S program would accomplish this.

Warner had a very low draft number so he decided to pick where he wanted to serve and joined the Navy. He went to boot camp and after that training was completed, he was sent to the Marines as a medical corpsman instead of into the V12S program. His unit was sent to Guadacanal in the South Pacific soon after it was taken by the United States. In those early days, they had nothing much in the way of ammunition and hardly enough gasoline to get one or two planes in the air because they were so far from supply sources. They did have guns and there was a lot of hand-to-hand combat, but Warner made the decision to never carry one.

During his time in the service, he saw many bad things, but it was an exciting time and it whetted his appetite for medicine. While on Guadacanal, he sustained a small shrapnel wound injury that became infected and spread. He was still interested in the V12S program, had taken the test and was eligible. However, the Commanding Officer refused a request for transfer back to the United States. Eventually, he was sent back to San Diego because of his injury. While in San Diego, the V12S program was offered again in Los Angeles so he went to USC and took the test again, became eligible and accepted into the program. He was accepted at George Washington University in Washington, D.C. From then on, there was no doubt that he was going to go to medical school as long as possible because the more he learned the more he loved it.

*   *   *   *

Glenn and Helen Camozzy were married when he was a freshman in medical school. They had a small monthly income from his service time and continuing education. Like so many young people at that time, Helen and Glenn thought they could get by on $100 a month. They had been high-school sweethearts and were married on December 31, 1944, in Ellensburg, Washington. Glenn told me, "Helen has always been the most instrumental thing in my life, supporting me and pushing me. We have been blessed. Some people might say it's been a struggle, but it hasn't been hard—it's been fun. Many material things others might expect were not important to us. We didn't then nor now miss a lot of creature comforts and material possessions. It has been an incredible partnership for over fifty years."

They knew that, eventually, they wanted to come back to the West Coast. While in school and in his graduate training, Warner was offered some really good positions with important work, but they would have had to live in Washington, D.C., or Chicago. After he graduated from George Washington University Medical School, he was accepted as an intern at Southern General Hospital in San Francisco which was affiliated with a Stanford University program. There weren't enough doctors at that time in that area so the students were given a lot of responsibility. That had been his experience in medical school and in his early training. He had been in places where the students were given an unusual amount of responsibility, much more so than what is given to medical students today.

After finishing in San Francisco, he went to the Stanford affiliated hospital in San Mateo where he received training in internal medicine. Then, the government decided that he would be required to go back into the service because he was not a doctor when he was in the service and now that he had completed medical school and training, he owed time to the service. Like so many others who had served in World War II, there was the possibility that he would be called up for the Korean War. All of these men were trying to reestablish themselves in civilian lives that had been put on hold. The prospect that he would have to serve additional years was not a pleasant one.

The Warners left California at that time with additional military service a possibility. They moved back to Washington State and found that Othello, Washington needed a doctor. There was an army base located near this small town and no doctor in the community. He had a general practice there for three years which was a great learning experience and he enjoyed his time in this community.

At the end of these three years, he was called up again by the Marines and told he would have to go to Korea because he still had not served in the military as a doctor. He went to Spokane, Washington, took his physical and was ready to go. Harry Truman was President at that time and he issued a directive stating that anytime served counted regardless of whether the individual was a non-commissioned or a commissioned officer. Because of this directive,

Warner was not required to go back into the service and could make some decisions about his future.

He decided he needed more training and went back to Othello to tell the community there that he was going to leave to pursue further education. At this time, he went to the University of Chicago to receive more training in surgery. The Deans Committee there gave him a residency without all the usual applications and recommendations. He was never sure how this worked out so well because usually there is a tremendous amount of red tape to go through before the hospital administrators will talk to an applicant and they are accepted or rejected. Normally, a person has to have many recommendations. All Warner did was walk in and say he wanted a job and they gave him a residency. He had excellent training under some wonderful surgeons. One in particular was Dr. Warren Cole who was considered one of the leading surgeons in the United States at that time.

After finishing training in surgery, Warner came back to Yakima, Washington, and did a combination of surgery and general practice. While in Chicago, he had been introduced to cancer work, both in pathology and surgery. The cancer therapy that had evolved was more trying to understand the disease than what was being done in treatment. He was stimulated to think in terms of understanding this disease; what causes cancer and why. Warner and his colleagues did many experimental things which, at that time, other people were not doing. They were allowed to do anything they wanted to do in research as long as they did not experiment on people.

It was 1959 and the practice in Yakima was good training, but it wasn't particularly fulfilling. One of the pathologists there suggested that perhaps Warner should think about pathology. He was told that Swedish Hospital in Seattle, Washington was one of the two best places in the nation for pathology. The other was in St. Louis. He corresponded with both of these hospitals. Swedish Hospital made the best offer so the Warners moved to Seattle.

After a couple of years, he missed the patient contact that was lacking in pathology. The hospital was looking for residents in radiation oncology. Residents in this discipline had to understand pathology and surgery among other things at that time. This presented him the opportunity to learn another specialty in addition to pathology. So he switched from pathology into radiation oncology.

It was an exciting time in the career of this young doctor. He had a passion for medicine and a hunger for knowledge. All of his training was leading him steadily toward his life work of caring for cancer patients. A collaboration with two outstanding researchers in the field of immunology furthered his conviction that there was still much to be learned about the human body and its response to disease.

CHAPTER 2

TUMOR INSTITUTE

It was an exciting time for Dr. Warner because he was seeing positive responses to new therapies. It was agreed that various kinds of immunotherapy procedures should be undertaken at the Tumor Institute. Bacillus-Calmette-Guerin (BCG) was tried to stimulate the immune system and it was extremely successful. Positive results were observed in many patients.

BCG is a weakened strain of the tuberculosis bacterium and has been safely used throughout the world since the 1940s as a vaccine against tuberculosis. However, it was still considered experimental by the FDA for use in the treatment of cancer. It was on what is called the Investigative New Drug List (IND).

BCG was normally administered by scarification. This procedure consisted of scratching a grid on the skin and applying the BCG in that area. This was covered with a patch for twenty-four hours. Side effects were minimal. Patients reacted as they would to any vaccination; running a slight fever for a day sometimes feeling flu-like symptoms for a short period of time.

Warner spent more and more time on this approach to the treatment of cancer. The immunologic section at the Tumor Institute of Swedish Hospital Medical Center was founded. This seemed like a huge step in the right direction in finding better and more humane methods of therapy.

Along with the immunotherapy program, various chemotherapy agents were utilized. All of these chemotherapy agents are derivatives of nitrogen mustard gas that destroys the reproductive capacity of the cells. This happened whether the cells were normal or abnormal. No attention was paid to the damage to the normal cell system. As a result, people on this treatment didn't last long. With such destructive techniques, the results were many times poorer then doing no treatment. It became obvious that there was a need for something else that would be more supportive to the patient. The natural way to do this would be an immunotherapeutic approach.

As more and more people became interested and more and more money was spent on research, it was found that, indeed, there are many mechanisms the body uses to keep itself well and protect itself against the constant change of cancer cells that occur in every person. When Warner began to learn how to control those mechanisms with the use of interferons, interleukins, the tissue necrosis factor, and other biologic response modifiers, he began to find that it was possible to alter the course of the illness biologically. This led to the current concept of the immunotherapy approach to the treatment of cancer.

At the same time, Dr. Orliss Wildermuth, then Director of the Tumor Institute, encouraged the staff to study more of the effects of other measures and try to find out why some patients lived longer than others did. Among other things, it was found that patients who lived longer were people who were non-compliant. They did not always follow the treatment programs advised. After further study, it was found that smaller doses of medication or different routes or methods or speeds of administration altered the effects of the treatment.

*   *   *   *

It was at this time in his career that Warner began work with Drs. Karl Erik and Ingegerd Hellstrom. The Hellstroms had done considerable work on lymphocyte physiology in Sweden and they brought that knowledge with them to the United States. (See Chapter 19 on the Immune System and Immunotherapy for an explanation of lymphocytes.)

Warner's group at the Tumor Institute had been doing limited research on lymphocytes. They did observe that the tumors that showed the best response to treatment were markedly infiltrated with lymphocytes. This, plus previous knowledge they'd had with some lymphomas, some testicular, and some thyroid tumors, showed that if there were a large number of lymphocytes in them, the tumors would be less aggressive with a more favorable prognosis. Further efforts to study the lymphocytes were thwarted by lack of training in this area. The arrival of the Hellstroms came at a most welcome time and their collaboration continued for many years.

The Hellstroms came to Seattle because at that time major immunotherapy work was being done at the University of Washington by Richmond Prehn, Ph.D., considered to be the father of immunotherapy in Seattle. He was developing a program to show that he could make animals become allergic to their own tumors. When he reinjected the tumor into the animal, the animal had antibodies against that tumor and would reject it. This idea was found to be immediated by the lymphocytes.

When the Hellstroms arrived in Seattle, they began their research at the University of Washington. They also taught classes on immunotherapy and continued to do this even after they had moved their research to Fred Hutchinson Cancer Research Center (FHCRC). Unfortunately, access to clinical material and patients were not available at the University of Washington. They heard of the work Warner was doing at the Tumor Institute so they contacted him, explained their problem, and their association with Warner began. Warner was able to provide clinical material and patients to further their study.

The Hellstroms had extensive knowledge about lymphocytes so the team melded together well in setting up a program to decide exactly what the function of the lymphocytes were and how they worked. That launched a general theory the Hellstroms developed. Their studies demonstrated that lymphocytes that were sensitized against the tumor and then mixed with the tumor cell in a separate culture dish destroyed the tumor. If lymphocytes from other tumors were used, this had no effect, showing there was a specificity of lymphocytes for the particular tumor. This was called the colony inhibition test.

In Warner's practice, he began seeing patients in various stages of their disease who had received different types of treatment. The affect on their lymphocytes was monitored to see if a reason for a difference in response could be found. Warner found that if the PH (acid/alkaline balance) of the solutions could be changed, this had a big affect on the cancer cell in the presence of the lymphocyte. However, the change in the PH could not be tolerated in humans. Dr. Hans Sjorgren, Dr. Ingegerd Hellstrom's brother, showed in his work that there were many ways you could manipulate the tumor and adversely affect its growth, but that it could not be done in humans because it was too toxic.

It was apparent that the lymphocytes were the cells responsible for the immune system. Warner supplied material for these tests and checked every possible tumor. He had the largest list of tumors of anyone in the area and was able to show that this lymphocyte was specific for every type of tumor checked. He was also able to show that there was recognition by the body of a non-cell situation. In other words, the foreign material in the tumor cell made the body realize it wasn't normal tissue and through the lymphocytes, started a response that, in some instances, killed the tumor. Because Warner had such a large number of patients and was able to prove the existence of a large number of lymphocytes in each individual tumor, it was possible to set the standard for future studies.

Together, Warner and the Hellstroms looked at lymph nodes and found that some contained large amounts of certain lymphocytes, which later were identified as T-cells that were trying to destroy the tumor. At this time in their collaboration, it was not recognized what was happening. Later, they saw that there were great amounts of lymphocytes in the neighboring lymph nodes. The ones that had large amounts of lymphocytes evidently were able to keep the tumor under control and the patients did better. Also, if they took the lymphocytes out of those lymph nodes and incubated them with the tumor, they were far more toxic to the tumor then others collected in other areas.

Small steps like these led to other things the Hellstroms were skilled at such as measuring the lymphocyte doses. Now it is known that the results have to do with interferon and interleukins. The hormone-like materials given off by the lymphocytes make them immunologically very powerful in regulating the body's response against disease. With the immunology aspect becoming more plausible, there were many indicators that made this a common sense approach to cancer therapy. It would seem to be a better approach then the destructive techniques that had been used up to this time.

*   *   *   *

It was about this time, 1975, that Cesar Milstein and Georges Kobler announced their discovery of monoclonals. They were conducting their research at the laboratory of Molecular Biology in Cambridge, England. The technology was simple. They created what they called a hybridoma by fusing an antibody producing B-cell from a mouse with a mouse cancer cell known as myeloma. This hybrid cell produced the specificity of an antibody producing cell and the mouse cells could forever manufacture the critical immune protein.

There were high hopes for the use of monoclonals against cancer over twenty years ago that are discussed later in this book. A limited understanding of immune function at that time led to premature beliefs that the use of monoclonal antibodies could be the knock-out approach scientists were looking for. As usual, they were overly optimistic and one of the key problems has been the selection of the right antigen to target and then understanding exactly what the antigen does. Two decades of basic research and clinical trials have led to some successes in disrupting the behavior of cancer cells.

Dr. Ingegerd Hellstrom recognized rapidly that the monoclonal studies were very important work. She immediately began investigating and within a week she dropped the study of cell testing and individual cell cytology. The English methods of Milstein and Kobler showed more promise in trying to find ways to make antibodies against tumor. From then on, the Hellstroms' efforts were more in this direction. Tumor tissue and blood from patients were obtained to inoculate them and see if anything specific could be done to regulate the growth of the tumor.

Work with the Hellstroms began in 1965. After the first five years, and the specificity of the lymphocytes had been proven, many practitioners thought that lymphocytes or immunotherapy would be the way to treat cancer. Everybody started off with enthusiasm on poorly planned and conceived programs. Immunotherapy measures such as vaccines and local irritants setting up an inflammatory reaction to tumors were used. Things of this nature were attempted in an effort to make the immune system strong enough to destroy the tumor, as if nothing more were needed. Of course, this approach fell flat on its face because cancer is such a complex mechanism. There were many other factors about cancer that were not known or considered. Instead of doing further studies, the treatment was rejected. There were those in the medical community who said immunotherapy would never have any part to play in medical treatment.

*   *   *   *

For the next ten years, the idea that immunotherapy had promising possibilities was relegated to the ash heap. The researchers had to prove the advantage of the immune system, that it was real. A number of different combinations were tried. The use of BCG was continued to see if there was any way the immune system could be stimulated to bring the lymphocyte counts up. Lymphocyte immune profiles were being used as the end point to show whether the patient was responding and whether the tumor disappeared. Many of these were in the days before anyone knew there was such a thing as tumor markers. Efforts were made to determine whether the tumor mass was reduced and if the patient got better clinically. These studies did show a positive difference.

Initially, tests were done on the patient to determine whether his lymphocytes were specific against his tumor only, or had any affect on tumors in other areas. Was there any cross relationship? It was proven that there was no cross relationship. At that time, investigators had no idea about cytokines or hormones from the lymphocytes that were responsible for all the activity.

It was only after Milstein's work was applied to the lymphocytes that it was realized there were many more things about lymphocytes needing to be learned. These extra studies occupied a great deal of time. It was hoped that through the hybridoma technique, an antibody could be manufactured. It was felt that this would significantly influence the disease.

Working with melanoma patients in 1979, Warner and the Hellstroms began to find that the number of antigens on the surface of a melanoma cell identified that cell as being a melanoma cell. Eight different antigens in all the tumor cells were classified. Dr. Ingegerd Hellstrom's work was largely responsible for this discovery. No matter what the melanoma cell was, one of these eight antigens would be expressed by the melanoma cell. Then it was possible to manufacture antibodies against those antigens.

About this time, it was noticed in some of the ongoing studies that every once in awhile, for reasons that were unexplainable, the tumor cultures would die out. There was no explanation as to why this happened except that the serum to incubate the tumor cells was being obtained from normal donors. Dr. Karl Hellstrom was frustrated as to what this discrepancy might be. Then he very meticulously went through the tests to see if there was any common denominator. He discovered that every time the donor of the serum was a black person the tumor culture died off. It was known that blacks did not have melanoma except on the whites of their hands, in their mouths, or in other hidden parts of their bodies. Dr. Hellstrom reasoned they must have something in their blood stream that might be responsible for killing the cells. This presented interesting possibilities and called for further investigation.

CHAPTER 3

MELANOMA STUDY

Permission and a grant from the National Cancer Institute (NCI) to study the effect of plasma from black donors on patients with melanoma were received. Representatives from the NCI were sent to Seattle to help set up the program at Fred Hutchinson Cancer Research Center (FHCRC). Apparently, this grant was funded with some reluctance because the prevailing attitude at the NCI was that chemotherapy was the only way to treat melanoma patients. This was in spite of the fact that John J. Constanzi, M.D., at M.D. Anderson Medical Center in Houston, Texas and a number of other people had been showing for years that no matter what combination or how it was administered there was no way that DTIC (dimethyl triazeno imidazole carboxmide) and other chemotherapy agents had any effect on the growth of melanoma cells.

Patients admitted into the protocol at FHCRC were randomized, one group with DTIC as against a group with black plasma. Another group received BCG scarification on the skin plus the black plasma. This treatment was administered for a full year. The University of Washington started out with a similar separate study, but, eventually, the two programs were put together.

Principal investigators were Drs. Glenn Warner, Peter Wright and Karl Erik and Ingegerd Hellstrom. Dr. Irving Bernstein was also on the committee. Dr. Bernstein was affiliated with Children's Hospital in Seattle and was a close friend of Peter Wright. BCG was listed at the FDA as an Investigative New Drug (IND) and Bernstein held permission for its use. Dr. Robert Jones was asked to be on the committee because of his position at the University of Washington as Associate Professor of Surgical Oncology along with a Dr. Ross Prentice. Other than coming periodically to some of the meetings and offering advice, Jones, Prentice and Bernstein had little to do with patient selection, obtaining material or the actual work.

At the end of the first year, the investigating group was asked to present its data and this was done before Dr. Don Thomas and Dr. Dennis Donohue. Drs. Peter Wright, Karl Erik and Ingegerd Hellstrom and Glenn Warner presented their findings. Drs. Thomas and Donohue concluded the study had to be flawed; that it must have been manipulated because there wasn't enough incidence of serum hepatitis in the amount of plasma transfusions given over a full year. They came to this conclusion because of the difference in the usual number of cases of hepatitis that would normally occur with this many transfusions.

There were two cases of hepatitis that were symptomatic enough to recognize a problem. If there were others, it was never known because of the lack of any evidence. Symptoms of hepatitis would be abnormal liver function, jaundice and liver swelling. Thomas and Donohue stated that because there were not the number of cases of hepatitis to be expected that somehow the investigators had altered the administration of the material or apparently never gave it. Thomas and Donohue also suspected that the group must have known the names of the patients or that they did not give the treatment according to the protocol. It was reported to be a non-study and stopped.

This protocol was what is called a blind-study and a code is needed in order to analyze the results. After the study was completed, Warner needed to know which patients had received the black plasma and which ones had ordinary plasma from white donors and the other combinations. However, he could not get the code. Ross Prentice, Ph.D., a statistician at the University of Washington, had the code and would not release it. It was three or four years later before Warner could get Prentice to release this information. This was troubling because Warner had every right to see the results of the protocol in which his patients were involved.

*   *   *   *

After the project was disbanded, it is believed that in less than a year all of those in the University group except for one or two had died and the others have subsequently died. The only way this information was available was through Warner's patients who were friends of those on the University part of the project. In the Tumor Institute group, there were a large number still alive at the five year level. Survival rate was about 70%. There has been a slow attrition of that group but not appreciable. Now at the end of more than fifteen years more then half of the approximately 75 Warner patients on the black plasma and BCG are still alive.

However, it was felt that Sera therapy (which this study was termed when it was presented to the American Society of Clinical Oncology (ASCO) in Arizona) was not a legitimate way to treat patients. Reasons given were the dangers of hepatitis and a number of other things that really had no bearing on the outcome of the program. This study was never mentioned again, never given any notoriety and there was never a suggestion that it was of value. Warner did try to show that it made a big difference. He was handicapped to prove his beliefs because he was not able to take care of patients and do the research work that was necessary to prove that the program was beneficial. It seems difficult to believe that this promising approach to melanoma therapy was dismissed without further investigation.

In retrospect, Warner wondered how much the influence of diet, vitamins and the concerns he and his staff had for their patients along with the compassionate care given helped in their ability to fight their disease. This was in marked contrast to what was done at the University. For this group, there was no nutritional support, nothing about vitamins and the treatment was done in a sterile clinic setting. The patients were merely numbers in the protocol study. Knowing what is now known about mind/body relationships, one wonders how much influence the person's mental attitude toward the treatment contributed to his well being.

In essence, the above is the melanoma project as conducted at FHCRC. It would be good to go back and review the protocol again because of the significant number of patients still alive, which is most unusual. Warner has always believed that much could have been learned from this study and it should not have been abandoned. He told me of several patients who, in his opinion, would not be alive today without the benefit of this experimental treatment.

*   *   *   *

One example would be P.P.C. who was diagnosed with malignant melanoma in 1970. A physician in Tacoma, Washington excised a mole on her leg in a simple office procedure. No follow-up care was recommended. By September 1971, the cancer had progressed to the lymph gland in her right groin.

This patient was a beautiful young woman, talented in singing and had moved to Boston to attend the Conservatory of Music there. With the recurrence of her melanoma, she was referred to a team of Harvard specialists at Massachusetts General Hospital. Dr. Terry McIneny, surgeon, declared his intentions of "going for broke" and performed radical, disfiguring surgery. The patient was never told what if any long-range benefits were hoped for by the surgeon. She did receive some follow-up care, but her confidence in the advice given to her completely broke down when repeated attacks of abdominal pain and flu-like symptoms in the Fall of 1972 were brushed off as stress.

In pain and very ill, Patty returned home in March 1973 and subsequently had surgery to remove a tumor in her small intestine. Her family physician referred her to Warner and he recommended she participate in the melanoma protocol. Even though this would be a blind study and she would be taking her chances as to the treatment she would receive, she believed it was her only chance. The only other medically acceptable choice of treatment would have been radiation and/or chemotherapy and her chance of full recovery would have been minimal.

When the code was finally broken, it was revealed that Patty was one of the lucky ones who received the plasma of black donors in combination with BCG. There can be no dispute that she had widely disseminated melanoma with a very poor prognosis for survival. She has had no recurrence of cancer and since 1989 she has lived in Tallahassee, Florida, with her husband.

*   *   *   *

A report of this study titled "Serotherapy of Malignant Melanoma" was published in *Progress in Cancer Research and Therapy, Volume 6* titled *"Immunotherapy of Cancer: Present Status of Trials in Man."*

The listed authors of this article were Peter W. Wright, Karl Erik Hellstrom, Ingegerd Hellstrom, Glenn Warner, Ross Prentice and Robert Jones. Acknowledgement for support and varied contributions were given to Dr. William Hutchinson, Fred Hutchinson Cancer Research Center, Dr. Roger Moe, University of Washington, Dr. Dennis

Donohue, Puget Sound Blood Center, Dr. H. Clark Hoffman, Swedish Hospital, and Dr. Edmund R. Clarke, Jr., Group Health Cooperative of Puget Sound, Seattle, Washington.

The summary of this article reads as follows: "The effect of administration of 'unblocking' plasma from normal black donors was compared to that of control Caucasian plasma in a prospective, randomized, double-blind trial in patients with stage II (regional lymph node involvement) and stage III (disseminated) melanoma. Stage II patients and stage III patients with no clinically evident disease at randomization received plasma and BCG scarification on alternate weeks. Stage III patients with non-resectable disease received the same immunotherapy, combined with systemic chemotherapy (DTIC). A conventional nonimmunotherapy control group was included in the first year of study. One hundred and eight evaluable patients (58 stage II and 50 stage III patients) were studied. No difference in progression rate or survival was observed in patients receiving unblocking plasma compared to control plasma. Similarly, no differences have been observed when patients receiving immunotherapy were compared with patients in a nonimmunotherapy control group. The number of patients included in the study to date have been too small, however, to exclude potential treatment differences of substantial magnitude."

It is obvious from the prior discussion in this chapter that Warner did not agree with the above summary even though his name was on the article as one of the authors. He was not able to make his own analysis of the results until some years later when he was able to get the code of the double-blind study. Only then did he discover how well his patients did who received plasma from black donors in combination with BCG. The trial did not continue long enough to show the real benefits. Was there too much prejudice against it from the examiners? And at what cost to future melanoma patients because it was abandoned?

CHAPTER 4

CONTROVERSY AT THE TUMOR INSTITUTE

Warner felt very comfortable with the developing program and hopeful about the future until Wildermuth retired and Dr. Donald Tesh became the new Director of the Tumor Institute. Up until that time, there had been no objections to the treatments he recommended for his patients. In fact, there were many reasons to be optimistic about what he was learning about this disease and how to control it.

The atmosphere at the Tumor Institute changed after the retirement of Wildermuth. Certain individuals from Fred Hutchinson Cancer Research Center wanted to take over the Tumor Institute and there were discussions on how this could be implemented. The governing board at Swedish Hospital Medical Center and doctors involved wanted it to remain a treatment center separate from FHCRC. The Tumor Institute was becoming internationally known as a training center for cancer therapy even though they did not do as much research. Their work was in a clinical setting with patients and the doctors were learning patient responses to treatment all the time. After much discussion and some hard feelings, the Tumor Institute did remain separate and continued to train residents. Because of this decision, they were an integral part of the birth of immunotherapy as a cancer treatment in Seattle.

All of this progress took a step backward with the ensuing controversy that ultimately resulted in Warner resigning. I have never been able to ascertain the person or persons who were determined to shut down Warner's practice. I do know the name of the doctor who requested an inspection of his practice by the FDA and I will discuss this later. There certainly was a division of opinion amongst medical personnel as to whether Warner should be allowed to continue with immunotherapy.

Warner's recollection was that the controversy began when Swedish Hospital instituted investigational reviews by peer review groups in the hospital. In other words, all the research projects had to be approved by a group of physicians who reviewed each proposed project. This overview would make sure that all of the treatment programs met whatever regulations were in place at the time. This seemed like a good idea except there were not many regulations in existence because this was a new concept.

Another change was that the requirement for informed consent began at this time. Any time a patient had any kind of experimental procedure they had to be fully informed. Informed consent would explain the recommended treatment, explain any possible side effects, and that the patient could withdraw from the program at any time; also, that a certain amount of the experimental therapy would not be charged to the patient. To make it even safer for the patient, each would be given a copy of every research project in which he was participating. The patient could then decide whether to go on the treatment recommended.

Dr. Peter Wright pointed out to the surveillance committee that Warner had been using BCG for cancers other than melanoma since the melanoma protocol at FHCRC. You could buy BCG and other similar agents legitimately in all pharmacies and medical supply houses without any special permission. There were no restrictions on its use. It is what the FDA calls off-shelf use. When a drug has been approved for one specific use, such as BCG for tuberculosis, it can be used for other diseases, such as cancer, even though the FDA considers that experimental. In spite of this, Wright pointed out that the treatment program Warner was using for melanoma patients in the study at FHCRC was now being made available to any patient who wanted to be on this particular project.

*   *   *   *

Warner believed the immunotherapy approach was more successful then the conventional approach and he was already incorporating other things he had found to be helpful in evaluating patients: such as, nutrition, vitamins, exercise and spiritual help. He found these things were significant in producing a favorable response to therapy. Healing of patients improved by incorporating all of these things in their treatment. All of these factors seemed to be just common sense approaches to making the patient stronger.

Warner also gave conventional therapies as they were generally prescribed at that time because he was not aware that lower doses would be effective. Eventually, with the addition of other supportive measures, he began to find his patients doing much better. He was trying to find measurements that would tell him if his patients were doing well. That is how Drs. Karl Erik and Ingegerd Hellstrom became involved. With their work, they would determine lymphocyte activity and specificity of the patient's lymphocytes against his particular tumor, but not against a tumor of similar variety in someone else. This was true because of the different genetic makeup in each patient.

With this project ongoing, it was decided that the peer review group should meet and review the therapies offered by Warner. Drs. Quin DeMarsh, Peter Wright and a number of other people were on the committee. They reviewed the program and decided the therapies were experimental and had not been proven to be of value.

The melanoma project at FHCRC had been rejected and Warner was ordered to discontinue his immunotherapy program. The committee decided that immunotherapy did not have anything to offer in the future and, in their opinion, the Hellstrom's work had not proven anything of value. This statement was made apparently without its being aware of the many experiments and findings that had already been developed on the immunotherapy of cancer and individual tumors. The Hellstroms studies did show the effectiveness of the response and were considered the seminal articles to refer to in planning further work or obtaining an understanding of this approach to therapy. In other words, they were considered to be among the leaders in the field at that time.

About this time, Wright requested a letter from Drs. Karl Erik and Ingegerd Hellstrom regarding their association with Warner. Their response is important as it verifies the important work these doctors were conducting in collaboration. It reads as follows and the underlining is the Hellstroms.

*   *   *   *

"March 2, 1979
Dr. Peter Wright
Fred Hutchinson Cancer Research Center
1124 Columbia
Seattle, Washington 98104
Dear Peter:

"A couple of days ago, you asked us to clarify our relationship with Dr. Glenn Warner, as it relates to a pending proposal from him (with our two names on the front page) which you are evaluating for Dr. DeMarsh's Committee. Let us make the following points.

"Our interaction with Dr. Warner has, essentially, been the same for the past ten years, when we first came in contact with him through one of our colleagues at the University of Washington; this was at a point when we were in desperate need for human material and had experienced many promises but very little in the form of what we needed (tumor material, blood lymphocytes and serum from cancer patients). The collaboration, which started in the late 1960s, has led to many papers, one of them, for example, listed among the Current Contents Publication Classics. Although our work in this area was, for quite a long time rather controversial, we are pleased to emphasize that the major conclusion reached, that of a cell-mediated immunity to antigens shared by human tumors of the same histological type, has been amply confirmed (for a discussion of this, with many references, see a recent article by Hellstrom and Brown in 'The Antigens', Vol. 5, pp. 1-82, 1979). Without our collaboration with Dr. Warner this work would never have materialized, and had it not been for this collaboration, and the hope that it will continue, we would probably not have left the University of Washington for the Hutchinson Cancer Research Center in 1975 (what we were lacking most of all, at the University was a close proximity to human tumor material). Of course, none of this work could have been carried out, had we not had proper approval from appropriate Human Subjects' committees; copies of two recent, still valid, such approvals are enclosed.

"As is apparent from what studies involving us have been approved by Human Subjects' committees, and also from our grant applications, on the basis of which our work is funded, our involvement in any human study is <u>exclusively</u> that of receiving tumor material, blood lymphocytes and sera. The only time we have been involved in actually treating patients (and then indirectly) was when the Immunotherapeutical Trials project (supported by National Institutes of Health Contract No 1 CV 64018 with you as co-principal investigator) was in effect; as you know, that project was terminated

March 31, 1978. <u>We have at no time made any promises, to clinicians or</u> <u>to patients, that 'immunological monitoring' of the patients with</u> <u>assays for cell-mediated anti-tumor immunity, blocking serum activ-</u> <u>ity, etc. does patients any good</u>—the patients contributing to such a study have done us a favor, by letting us study them, and would do themselves and other cancer patients a favor only if the studies would lead to development of clinically useful, immunological assays. As we have emphasized in several papers (e.g., Hellstrom and Hellstrom, Cancer Res. 39:649-650, 1979), clinically useful immunological assays remained to be developed, and our attitude has been more conserva- tive on that point than that of many of our fellow tumor immunolo- gists (e.g., Halliday, Thomson, Goldrosen). We do, of course, believe that immunological assays useful for routine monitoring of human cancer patients can be ultimately worked out (otherwise we would not spend our time working in the area), and we hope, in particular, that the monoclonal antibody approach offers a new possibility in this direction. (As you know, we recently completed a paper, on which Dr. Warner is one of the co-authors, showing the production of mono- clonal antibody to an antigen present on a human melanoma, the anti- body having a very high specificity for the antigen and having a titer of approximately 1:10). Of course all the material procured by Warner and given to us is being used for our studies, and the findings obtained are being published (one would hardly be able to secure funding otherwise).

"As far as the advisability for Glenn Warner, or anyone else, of giv- ing human cancer patients BCG, we do not want to take any official stand since others are more competent than ourselves in doing so. We just want to emphasize again, that <u>we have personally never given</u> BCG to any cancer patient, or have planned to do so, and we have only at one point of time been involved in a clinical study, in which this was done; this was the Immunotherapeutical Trial, mentioned above, in which you were one of the two co-principal investigators.

"Let us emphasize, again, that Dr. Warner has been, and continues to be, a key person in our studies on human tumor antigens and the host response to them. The amount of time he has spent, not only in procuring material but also in making it possible to study the same patients over a long time period is exceptional. Investigators at most universities and cancer centers have not had the opportunities Warner has given us for studying human tumor immunity and we have felt some friendly envy from many colleagues from other institutions who wished they had the same opportunities. Would Warner's role in providing material terminate, the attractiveness of Seattle for us as a place to work would decrease, since many here have, in the past, given us promises about what human material we could get, but few have 'delivered', and none has done so to the extent of Dr. Warner.

"Please let us know, if any further information is needed, and we would be happy to provide this information either in writing, or orally, to whoever wants to have it.

Yours Sincerely,

(Signed) Karl Erik Hellstrom, M.D.,

Professor of Pathology

Ingegerd Hellstrom, M.D.,

Professor of Microbiology/Immunology"

*   *   *   *

In spite of the endorsement of the Hellstroms, the committee decided that the department of immunotherapy would have to be disbanded and Warner would be required to use only medical oncology considered acceptable at that time. The patients on treatment would have to be returned to their general practitioners.

Swedish Hospital pharmacy had been making up Warner's medications over the years so they knew what treatments were being used. The medications were put up in capsules to use in various kinds of treatments. They were labeled to be safe and good for certain specific experimental studies. Warner was simply expanding the field to encompass all of the malignant tumors to monitor the response of patients. Would it be any different from the few who had been studied extensively such as those with melanoma and lung tumors?

Later the FDA inspected his treatments and pointed out that the material being used had been obtained from veterinary sources. It was a fact that the purity and quality was the same as any medications used in humans and the preparation was quality controlled. The peer review committee tried to show that this was using inferior material on human beings.

All of this was an attempt to shut down the immunotherapy approach. The committee said it should only be done at the University of Washington or the Fred Hutchinson Cancer Research Center. Anything that was done in the future would have to be reviewed by professors at the University.

Warner did not like this evaluation, but the biggest thing he did not like was that he would have to discontinue treatments he thought had been effective in a large number of patients. They would have to be sent back to their general practitioners without any follow-up therapy. That was his main reason for saying he would prefer to take care of his patients in private practice rather then conform to some rules and regulations laid down to supposedly prevent misuse of experimental procedures. The decision of the peer review committee was not recommended in the FDA inspection report. It seems likely that this information was given only to the peer review group and no one paid much attention to it except those who wanted to use it as a reason to discontinue the immunotherapy approach.

On April 3, 1979, Dr. Warner was informed that the immunology program would be terminated within three months.

The whole controversy at the Tumor Institute concerned Dr. Warner's use of BCG because it was considered experimental. Warner had presented a protocol for its use but was turned down by the peer review committee. They directed him to do a randomized study, which he rejected. A randomized blind study would mean that half of the patients involved would receive BCG and half would receive placebos. His reason was that if he had a beneficial treatment he did not want to deny it to any of his patients.

In a subsequent chapter on BCG and the FDA you will see that there was nothing illegal about using BCG even though it was, and still is except for bladder cancer, on the Investigational New Drug list for use in cancer treatment.

Undoubtedly, Warner's biggest mistake was in not publishing the results of his success in the use of immunotherapy. He kept meticulous records and the medical community would have found it hard to ignore or discount the fact that his patients were benefiting from this approach if all the facts had been made public. In his defense, time was a mitigating factor as he had a tremendous patient load. The patient was always his main concern and he worked long hours trying to meet all their needs.

During this controversy, I was an active patient of Dr. Warner's and vitally interested in the continuance of his program. I wasn't satisfied that he was being treated fairly so I decided to do some investigating of my own.

CHAPTER 5

FDA AND BEYOND

On April 17, 1979 at approximately 4:00 P.M., I had a meeting with Dr. Donald Tesh, Director of the Tumor Institute at Swedish Hospital. I had requested this meeting so he could explain to me the action taken terminating the immunology program.

During our conversation, Dr. Tesh told me that Dr. Warner should not take this action personally because it came from a ruling by the FDA that BCG was being used illegally. The words he used were, "It is out of the hands of Swedish Hospital." He said there was an investigation by the FDA which found that Warner was not practicing under an IND or a protocol required when administering an experimental drug. Tesh did say that in all fairness to Warner, he had been using BCG long before an IND permit was required.

I decided to find out for myself what action the FDA had taken. My feeling at the time was that it was rather odd that the FDA would make an investigation of the use of BCG by Dr. Warner when he had been using it successfully for so long. I wanted to find out if someone at Swedish Hospital had instigated the investigation. Imagine my surprise to find out there had been no investigation at all.

I called the FDA in Seattle and talked to Ray Johnstone. He had no knowledge of any investigation of the use of BCG at the Tumor Institute. He was, however, very helpful. He took down all the information and said he would call me back. When he returned my call, he said that he had talked to Joyce Cremer in the Oncology Section in Washington, D.C., and she knew of no investigation. She made the statement that it was probably misleading if Dr. Tesh had told me that the FDA had forbidden Swedish Hospital to use BCG.

Joyce Cremer suggested I call Dr. John Pente at the National Cancer Institute in Washington. D.C. Also, she thought it might be helpful if I called the FDA, Bureau of Biologics in Washington, D.C. I had a daughter who lived in D.C. at that time and I gave her the information to pursue. Dr. Pente told her that Warner's treatment program was not being conducted under the National Cancer Institute so they would have no knowledge of it. She then talked to Mr. Cipriano at the Bureau of Biologics. He said the FDA had not issued any investigative report on the use of BCG as a treatment of cancer at Swedish Hospital or anyplace else. He said they did not have adequate studies to determine if BCG was effective, but they did not consider it harmful.

Mr. Cipriano went on to say that if Swedish Hospital had been buying BCG for Warner out-of-state, they would have to have an IND. If it was bought directly from a pharmacy in state, no IND is required. If an IND report had been required these many years, Swedish Hospital would have had to file a yearly progress report. The IND requirements are quite simple: a doctor must be administering it who has the proper credentials, must state how it is used and the protocol can be either patient control or historical control. The latter means that you do not have to randomize patients, but can report on all patients receiving the drug.

Mr. Cipriano said that I should check to see if there had been a regulatory action against Warner by the FDA. This is a long, careful investigation and would result in Warner being disqualified as being incompetent to administer an experimental drug. He said the FDA is very careful about taking regulatory action because they don't care much about being sued. Mr. Cipriano's final remark to my daughter was that it sounded like hospital politics to him.

My next step was to find out the name of the local investigator. It was Martha Brimm located in the Federal Office Building, Seattle, Washington. When I called her, I was told she was on vacation for a month. I asked to speak to someone who might give me information about her investigation. I was connected to a Mr. Zuber and I asked him for copies of any documents under the Freedom of Information Act pertaining to the use of BCG by Warner. He said this request would have to go through the usual endless channels of government.

Mr. Zuber was not particularly cooperative, but he did say that Martha Brimm had conducted an inspection, not an investigation, and it was in the process of being typed. I asked him if there had been a regulatory action against Warner and he said there had not. Since he seemed reluctant to give me information on the phone, I said there was just one more question and the answer was very important to me. *Had the FDA forbidden Swedish Hospital and Dr. Warner to use BCG in the treatment of cancer? Mr. Zuber said it had not.*

*   *   *   *

What I find impossible to believe is that in an effort to terminate Warner's program doctors would stoop to misrepresenting the facts and would have an absolute disregard for the hundreds of patients who were under the care of Warner. This was a physician who had given many years of dedicated service to the Tumor Institute.

The only explanation would seem to be that those who wanted to terminate Warner's program, for whatever reason, had to come up with something that would sound plausible to the Trustees of Swedish Hospital. Presuming them to be honest men, the Trustees accepted their statement that the FDA had declared Warner's use of BCG illegal and forbidden him to use it.

I requested the FDA inspection report under the Freedom of Information Act. When I received it, there were many parts deleted, but it stated very clearly that the inspection had been undertaken at the request of a doctor at the University of Washington and was not instigated by the FDA. The report did not come to any definitive conclusions. It stated that the FDA had no set policy on the use of BCG. The inspection was conducted reluctantly and certainly was not initiated by them. All of the events leading up to the termination of the immunology program at the Tumor Institute were extremely unsettling and affected Warner's patient care in a major way.

Peer review groups were set up to evaluate all the projects and decide which ones they would follow and which ones they would not. In review, they found Warner was using BCG on tumors other than melanoma after the melanoma project had been discontinued. At that time, he was informed that the permit to use BCG had been granted only to Dr. Irwin Bernstein and not to Peter Wright. Everyone assumed, as the principal investigator, he had been granted the right to use BCG on the melanoma project. Certain requirements were then set up for Wright; such as, signing up with the FDA and other hospital regulations. He at first refused to do so believing the requirements imposed certain limitations on his freedom to conduct research. He finally had to acquiesce when Mavis Rowley, one of the supervising officers for the peer review group, told him he had to comply or be removed from the Swedish Hospital staff.

Then Wright pointed the finger at Warner and said he was using BCG in many other ways than intended. Suddenly, the peer review group began looking at his therapies. Warner was using treatment programs that were a part of protocols done by the Southwest Oncology group under FDA approval. He was allowed, under this protocol, to use any combination of the drug he thought would be beneficial to the patient. He was attempting to adapt the drug and dosage to the patient instead of just treating a large number of patients with one agent. The peer review committee decided the treatments used by Warner were not of value even though he had found that if used in a certain way they were helpful and could influence the patient's well being.

Warner was asked to submit a protocol and he did. Dr. Malcolm Mitchell who was then at the University of Southern California reviewed the protocol. Mitchell replied in a letter that while he did not see the value in Warner's approach, it should be tried for a year or so to see if it was beneficial. After all, they were having very little success with the therapies they were using. Yet, DeMarsh and Wright and a number of others felt this was quackery and anything that was not done under their direction and contained chemotherapy was denying cancer patients a method of therapy that would be curative.

It came down to the point of almost an inquisition type of situation. They asked Warner to explain why he was doing all the various things that were parts of protocols as if he had been deliberately trying to make patients worse. Then they denied him the opportunity to continue to treat patients with non-specific immune therapy combinations. He was instructed to immediately return all patients to their previous doctors. All of the therapy had to be discontinued.

The peer review committee decided that the work with the Hellstroms was of no value to them and needed to be separated from anything the Tumor Institute and Swedish Hospital was doing. Warner was instructed to desist from using any further programs dealing with this approach to cancer therapy. He was directed to confine himself to a chemotherapy only approach. It was so restrictive that it was an obvious put down. So much so that he said, "Well, I can't do that and I'll leave the Tumor Institute and set up my own program."

All of this led to his resigning from the Tumor Institute and working out a deal to split the office space of the Tumor Institute in half. He would take his half for immunotherapy plus additional support programs and they would do the conventional therapy. There would be a common waiting room and records would be kept in the same files.

While all this was going on, his treatments of patients continued. After a year, it became obvious to other doctors at the Tumor Institute that Warner's patients were doing so much better than theirs that they could not mix them in the same waiting room. The nurses and receptionist would look at the patients and could tell which were Warner's patients and which were the patients of the other group. So Warner was asked to move although it came down to the fact that both programs had grown to a size where there was not enough space. Warner definitely needed more space to enlarge his program.

Warner was stunned by what had transpired. After a long and successful career at the Tumor Institute, he could hardly comprehend why he was suddenly surrounded by critics, and some of those critics he had considered to be his good friends. He had worked under Dr. Orliss Wildermuth for many years and excerpts from the following long letter written by Wildermuth details that association.

*   *   *   *

"September 25, 1980
"Re: Glenn A. Warner, M.D.
"TO WHOM IT MAY CONCERN:
"This is to verify that I have known Dr. Glenn Warner since the late 1950s when he entered the training program at the Tumor Institute of the Swedish Hospital in radiation therapy and general oncology as directed by and with the approval of the late Dr. Simon P. Cantril. The program was partially sponsored by the U.S. Public Health Service through the National Cancer Institute training program, and funds of the Tumor Institute and the Swedish Hospital. The program was for

three years and at the time Doctor Warner was in training there were four other residents in the program.

"Doctor Warner came to us from the pathology training program in Swedish Hospital where he had been for a one year refresher in pathology, prior to coming into radiation therapy. During the time he was in the radiation therapy program, he became associated with Dr. Dennis Donohue who at that time was a ranking member of the Northwest Cancer-Chemotherapy Regional Conference and Doctor Warner spent half days with him for the last year of his training program. Subsequent to that, he spent the following year in medical oncology with Doctor Donohue as his assistant and associate for the patients housed in the Swedish Hospital. It was at this time that Doctor Donohue was contemplating joining the Tumor Institute staff as a medical oncologist, but that did not come to fruition.

"Doctor Warner continued his interest in medical oncology even after taking his radiation therapy specialty Boards which he passed in the proper sequence of time, and as a member of the Tumor Institute staff he continued in this function, doing his radiation therapy in all aspects plus the chemotherapy, as was required for patient management in those days early in the development of cancer therapy when medical oncology as a specialty did not exist. It was not until the early 1970s that Doctor Warner became acquainted with Dr. Hans Sjorgren, now one of the Directors of immunology and immunotherapy at Karolinska Institute in Stockholm, Sweden. Doctor Sjorgren at that time was associated with the Hellstroms and is a brother of Mrs. Hellstrom. He was a ranking immunologist at that time and was working in cellular immunology with the Hellstroms.

"Working with Doctor Warner at the Northwest Research Foundation of those days, a good deal of basic immunology was carried out and various studies in laboratory works in cellular immunology were pursued. Doctor Warner worked with Dr. Hans Sjorgren until his return to Sweden some years later, and he studied extensively in immunology at that time. At Doctor Sjorgren's departure, and with the Hellstroms' joining the staff of the Fred Hutchinson Cancer Research Center, Doctor Warner changed his relationships and became the clinical arm for human application in the studies of the Hellstroms. The Hellstroms and Warner did several publications in outstanding journals, over their signatures. Doctor Warner at that time was probably one of the most knowledgeable people in clinical oncology as far as foundations in immunology were concerned.

"As time went on and as immunological attitudes improved and developed leads, studies were carried out at the Tumor Institute of the Swedish Hospital under Doctor Warner's direct supervision, with constant consultation with the Hellstroms. As a matter of fact, weekly conferences were held in the Tumor Institute. Many studies of considerable note were pursued and brought to fruition.

"At that time, the development of immunology in therapy did not bear any great fruit and there was much re-establishment of laboratory data to make it more applicable. During this time, however, Doctor Warner continued to function in his capacity as a radiation therapist on the Tumor Institute staff.

"It was not until 1975, or thereabouts, when the Tumor Institute moved into new quarters in the Arnold Building, that a physical separation could be made so that chemotherapy, which was now primarily under the supervision of Doctors Weber and Rivkin, could be placed in its own quarters and share certain facilities with Doctor Warner who also had his quarters for his immunological pursuits. This seemed to occupy the greater part of his time, so that it was impossible for him to have specific and continuing responsibilities in radiation therapy. It was therefore my decision that he spend his full time in immunology and give up supervision of patients in radiation therapy.

"Doctor Warner, however, continued to ask for radiation therapy for its immunologic effects under certain circumstances which were very specific and are very positively demonstrated in immunology.

Similarly, he used chemotherapeutic agents for the same effect on the immunological systems Some of these effects are poorly understood by the ordinary practicing physician and seem to be conflicting and an indication of poor judgment. However, if one learns about the development of immunology and its various ramifications today, the uses of these small doses of radiation and of chemotherapy are seen to be of great scientific import. With this background of Doctor Warner's training and development of expertise in fields of cancer management that were on the forefront of their development, namely chemotherapy before it was a medical specialty and immunology before it was an oncologic breakthrough, I will now proceed to comment on the letters that have been submitted condemning Doctor Warner's activities."

Dr. Wildermuth's letter goes on to discuss and refute specific charges against Dr. Warner in his treatment of patients.

In response to a statement in a letter from Dr. Lobb, then director of Swedish Hospital, Dr. Wildermuth says, "In regards to Dr. Lobb's letter. This is in response to a telephone call or letter from Doctor Lasher to Dr. Lobb on May 1, 1980. There is an incorrect statement midway in the first paragraph regarding the activities of the Research Civilians' Committee of the Swedish Hospital staff by Dr. Quin DeMarsh, and I paraphrase to say that he stated that the therapy Doctor Warner was using was inappropriate and it became outlawed by the FDA. This is not in line with the facts. Doctor Warner's programs were reviewed and approved by the Human Experimentation Committee or Research Civilians' Committee of the Swedish Hospital of which I was a member along with Dr. Quin DeMarsh. They were approved. Doctor Warner was dilatory in his compliance with the regular reports to the Human Experimentation Committee. He also fell into conflict with a member of the Fred Hutchinson Cancer Research Center that held the investigational number from the FDA for BCG and, unknown to him, was taken off approval and Doctor Warner was not punctual in pursuing the establishment of a number of his own. For this reason, he was asked to discontinue his activities until he complied with the requirements of the committee, namely having his own experimental number from the FDA and secondly, for getting his reports up to date as required.

"Finally, there is a statement in the last paragraph that Doctor Warner pushed immunotherapy in the treatment of cancer inappropriately to the exclusion of more acceptable methods. This is hearsay and not necessarily true if one considers from the standpoint of an immunologist the management of the patient rather than from the standpoint of a surgeon, radiotherapist, or chemotherapist.

"Referring to the letter dated April 21, 1980 by Dr. Tom Griffin, head of the Radiation Oncology Department at the University of Washington, to my knowledge Doctor Griffin did not appear on the scene in Seattle until after Doctor Warner was out of radiation therapy and in the immunological section of the Tumor Institute, so he had little chance to be more than aware of the name and reputation of Doctor Warner. Doctor Tesh came on the scene about the time of the move or shortly thereafter and had no knowledge of Doctor Warner's training or staff activities in the Tumor Institute prior to his coming on the scene. Doctor Tesh had very little contact with Doctor Warner except as a referring physician.

"The second paragraph contains a mistake again in the statement that 'proven methods were eliminated when Doctor Warner used immunological techniques in the treatment of advanced cancer'. There are no proven methods. There are only methods that are under investigation. Otherwise, there would be only one method of proper treatment of each case. The second statement, that BCG was experimental, refers only to the use of BCG in cancer. Its ability to stimulate the immune system is without refutation and its establishment as a part of medicine in the treatment of childhood leukemia and in the treatment of tuberculosis is of course beyond question. The statement that Doctor Warner did not obtain permission from the Human Subjects Review Committee of

Swedish Hospital is a mark of total ignorance of the fact. His research applications were filed with the Human Experimentation Committee in proper order and form. Doctor Warner, of course, did develop a philosophy and a system of blending the use of the stimulation of the patient's own system into the total program of management of patients with cancer and so the statement that his philosophy was out of line is true only in that it was out of line with those who are ignorant in the use of immunological procedures.

"The next letter (from Doctor Applebaum), is only a matter of personal opinion in a situation where the failure rate of cure is the same and continues to be the same since the 1930s in data published by the American Cancer Society and the National Cancer Institute. Or, stated in another way, the death rate per 100,000 for cancer of the breast has not changed in the last 30 years, indicating the need for an entirely new approach to the management of this disease for those who are not cured by the initial procedure. There is no evidence that postoperative radiation therapy cures any patients over the numbers cured by surgery alone. Radiation therapy, in my opinion, should not be given postoperatively, and this opinion is entertained by most data published on the use of radiation therapy as an adjuvant to surgery in the treatment of carcinoma of the breast.

"With respect to the letter from Dr. (name withheld by author), Professor of Surgery at the University of Washington, as usual this is highly inflammatory and totally the result of superficial thinking, hearsay, and repetition and magnification of errors. The letter stated that Dr. Glenn Warner is not a competent oncologist. If he means oncologist in the use of chemotherapy his training is early and extensive and continuous and, while he did not enter it in the usual fashion (namely through internal medicine) he did spend many years in his original training with Doctor Donohue who at that time was the foremost chemotherapist in the area, and he continued his activities in chemotherapy throughout his medical career in Seattle from that time on. To say that he had not practiced radiation therapy from the time of the therapy is so far from the truth I will comment no further, only refer you to my previous notes as to his actual participation at the Tumor Institute. (This doctor) then says there is well documented evidence of Doctor Warner's mismanagement, but he does not in any way show the cases to which he refers. (This doctor) was an obstructionist to the decrease in the radical surgery in carcinoma of the breast and he feels threatened by immunological entry into cancer therapy, in my opinion. His statement that potentially curable cases were denied proven therapy would have to be documented and I think in every case could be refuted by people who are more intellectual in their pursuit of rumors than (this doctor) has demonstrated. The case that he refers to in his final paragraph, wherein he states that the patient had late radiation therapy because she was held off from having early radiation therapy by immunology is a statement unsupported, only a rumor, and does not jibe with the facts as known in association with Doctor Warner in his care of patients. The fact that Doctor Warner offered these patients immunology was an indication of his desire and his continual study in striving to extend the care of these patients, even when failure from conventional chemotherapy, radiation therapy and surgery were predicted or evident.

"I am at a loss to understand the paragraph about Doctor DeMarsh forbidding Doctor Warner to do experimental immunotherapy. I have no idea under what circumstances this could have occurred. It certainly did not occur as a function of Doctor DeMarsh's activities as chairman of the Human Experimentation Committee as I was in all of those committee sessions and pronouncements, particularly when pertaining to members of my staff until Doctor Weber became chairman. At no time was Doctor Warner forbidden. He was admonished to get his reports in. He was admonished to pursue his own IND and, as far as I am aware, at no time during my sojourn as Director of the Tumor Institute until January 1979, any forbidding of Doctor Warner to pursue these studies in immunotherapy which have become so prominent in all the cancer centers throughout the United States and Europe. The last paragraph for comment is utterly unacceptable, should be stricken from any record, and only indicates the ignorance of the development of immunology that is being pursued throughout the United States and the lack of judgment in being able to evaluate its impact on the total treatment of patients.

"I think he (Warner) should pursue his areas of expertise and those are the care of the incurable patient with cancer with all the modalities that are available to the cancer therapist today, including nutrition, cytotoxic drugs, radiation therapy, immunologic therapeutic agents, and whatever will appear on the scene in the future that is of benefit to the patient for whom we have so little to offer with the conventions of surgery, radiation and cytotoxic drugs.
(Signed) Orliss Wildermuth, M.D."

*　　　　*　　　　*　　　　*

During the time that Dr. Wildermuth was Director of the Tumor Institute, he was completely supportive of Dr. Warners's approach to cancer therapy as evidenced by his letter. It was only after he retired and Dr. Tesh became the new director those attacks began.

I remember that during these turbulent times I remarked to Dr. Tesh that I thought the Tumor Institute was taking a giant step backwards. Because of the success of my own treatment with immunotherapy, I had bragged about this exciting new approach in the treatment of cancer.

Because of his desire to continue treating patients with the best therapies available, Warner moved his practice to the Cabrini Tower and took with him all but one patient. The husband of the patient who did not come with Warner said he realized it probably was the best treatment, but he thought his wife should stick with the University program because in the long run they would be closer to the truth about the best treatments. She began other therapy and, unfortunately, two or three years later she died. She had been under Warner's care for a long period of time prior to changing treatment. She had a good quality of life and, in his opinion, she died from overtreatment, which is often the case.

The Northwest Oncology Clinic was born at Cabrini Tower. Originally, they had 1400 square feet and eventually grew to 3200 square feet. The practice grew and prospered. It was an operation that gave total patient care starting with nutrition, exercise, meditation and spiritual help plus whatever conventional therapy had been proven to be of value. Over the years, the patient load grew and the successful treatment and prolongation of life was evident in the fact that there was a tremendous backlog of patients who are still alive many years later with and without treatment as a result of this approach.

It was at this time that Helen Warner joined the staff and worked with her husband every day. In addition to other duties, she was the official hostess. She greeted patients with her beautiful smile and many hugs. She transformed the waiting room into a happy gathering place where patients exchanged stories and information instead of a place of intimidation and fear. Hard to believe, but true.

PART II

PERSECUTION BY THE STATE MEDICAL BOARD

CHAPTER 6

MEDICAL QUALITY ASSURANCE COMMISSION (MQAC) & GLENN WARNER

In spite of a thriving practice and hundreds of satisfied patients, the same group that was instrumental in terminating the immunology program at the Tumor Institute of Swedish Hospital remained determined to put Warner out of business. Why? Was it because he was attracting so many patients who had failed these doctors' treatments? Were they fearful that their approach to cancer therapy would, in the long run, be proved wrong? Could it have been because he was not part of the mainstream of the medical community?

It seems possible that these doctors could not stand his success. I'm sure they believed that when he left the Tumor Institute his practice would diminish and he would slowly fade away. Instead, the majority of his patients followed him when he moved. His practice kept steadily growing as the word spread of how well his patients were doing and the quality of life they had while undergoing treatment. Many patients came to him after failing radiation and/or chemotherapy hoping that somehow he could save their lives—and he often did. Other patients came with a referral from their primary care physicians. Certainly, those doctors didn't believe he was a danger to the public health.

I do not believe that any of the doctors involved thought he was doing anything harmful. So, then, for some reason it became a personal vendetta and that is hard to fathom because Glenn Warner was such a gentle, soft-spoken man.

In medical journals and lay publications so much was being written about the importance of the immune system. A new field called psychoneuroimmunology was emphasizing the connection of the body and the mind in the process of healing. Yet so many doctors rejected this approach and still adhered strictly to surgery, radiation and chemotherapy as the only acceptable treatments.

It was in 1985 that Warner was alerted to the fact that a complaint had been filed against him by another doctor. This was addressed to the Medical Disciplinary Board (subsequently changed to the Medical Quality Assurance Commission (MQAC). He was not notified of this action, but through his lawyers found that the complaint was considered at a meeting on February 15, 1985. His practice was reviewed and the charge was dismissed. Warner concluded that he had been cleared of any wrongdoing and did not change his methods of caring for his patients.

What happened next was totally unexpected. On May 19, 1989, four years after the original complaint, a statement of charges by the MQAC was made against Glenn Warner, but not received by him until sometime later. What followed is an unbelievable seven years of hearings and court appearances. Although the MQAC and the Attorney General's office continually assured Warner of his right to due process, as events unfolded it became apparent there was no such thing when charged by a State Commission. They scheduled, then canceled meetings and hearings, changed venues without notifying the parties involved in a timely manner and rejected the findings and conclusions of the Administrative Law Judge (ALJ) they had appointed.

Most doctors would have had to give up without a fight because of the enormous legal expenses. Warner's legal costs of over $400,000 were paid by friends and patients and in the end it was all for naught because it was clearly demonstrated that if a doctor is targeted by the MQAC there is no way he can possibly win. The Commission is judge, jury and prosecutor. They answer to no one: not the citizens of the State, the legislature, the courts or even the Governor. And, of course, they have a bottomless pit of money

Following is how the actions against this intelligent, caring and compassionate doctor unfolded.

On May 26, 1989, Warner received a notice from Wilhelm Dingler, Assistant Attorney General, that a Settlement hearing would be held at the office of the Attorney General on July 7, 1989. This hearing was never held. Instead, on this date the Attorney General's office notified Warner that a Formal Hearing would be held on September 11, 1989 at Providence Hospital, Seattle.

Meetings before the MQAC are open to the public and we were attempting to notify the many people who wanted to attend. It was difficult to do this when the MQAC changed times and places in what seemed to be a capricious manner. Do you suppose this was a deliberate attempt to keep Warner's supporters away from the hearings?

Four days before the scheduled September 11th hearing, I called the MQAC to verify the time and place and was told the hearing had been canceled. I called Wilhelm Dingler and he informed me that the location had been changed and that he had asked for a continuance. Warner was not notified until after I called that the hearing had been postponed. This was costly to him as he had already canceled all of his appointments with patients for the week.

At this time, with Warner's permission, I wrote a letter to 350 of his patients asking them to write a letter of support and send it to the MQAC. Not only did all of them respond but family and friends wrote letters, too. It was an incredible demonstration of faith in their doctor. I wish I could publish all of them. I have selected a few to give you a sample of how these informed, intelligent patients felt about their treatment. (These letters are in Part III, Chapter 18, titled Success Stories.) A representative of the MQAC subsequently informed me that they would not read any of the letters that flooded their office. Their reason was that it might prejudice them in Warner's favor. Isn't that amazing? Who would be better qualified to evaluate the quality of care than the patients?

Throughout the following years the support of Warner's patients never wavered. They showed up in large numbers at every hearing, filled courtrooms and spilled out into hallways, even picketed the MQAC offices in Olympia, Washington and in front of the courthouse in Seattle on numerous occasions. And they continued to write letters to everyone they thought might influence the outcome of the proceedings, all to no avail. The patients' rights were never considered.

Warner was notified on October 13, 1989, that a hearing before the MQAC would be held November 13, 1989 at the Seattle Center, later changed to the Radison Hotel in Tacoma, Washington without telling anyone. Warner's counsel of choice could not be present on November 13th and a continuance was requested which was denied. This necessitated the expense of taking the request to court where the continuance was granted.

Eventually, an undated letter was received from Mary Turner, Executive Officer of the MQAC rescheduling the hearing for February 15-17, 1990 and March 22-24, 1990 at the Tacoma Sheraton Hotel in Tacoma, Washington, later changed to the Bellevue Concourse in Bellevue, Washington. In January 1990, Mary Turner did not give me any reason, but informed me that she was not sure the hearing as scheduled would take place. It did not and was rescheduled to April 23-28, but this meeting also was never held.

*   *   *   *

The original charges filed against Warner were so vague that it would have been impossible to prepare a defense. The MQAC, represented by the Attorney General's office, was bound by its own rules of procedure to make full disclosure. Repeated requests to the Attorney General's office by Warner's attorney for the specific nature of each charge were ignored.

At this time, Warner's attorney filed a motion before the MQAC to have the charges dismissed and the motion was set to be heard on March 14, 1990. Shortly before the hearing date, counsel received a call that the hearing would not take place until March 20th. The reason for the delay this time was that the Attorney General's office failed to submit its reply brief until 11:00 A.M. on the day of the hearing. This made it impossible for the Commission to circulate the brief to the panel that was going to hear the motion. The motion for dismissal was denied on March 22, 1990. The Commission did, however, instruct the Attorney General's office to provide a more definitive Statement of Charges by March 30, 1990.

Because the Attorney General's office did not respond to the directive of the MQAC, legal counsel took the matter to King County Superior Court. The Court entered an order staying Warner's hearing until such time as the Superior Court could have a full hearing to consider the constitutional issues raised concerning the MQAC's failure to follow state law in issuing charges against the defendant, and to provide him with adequate notice of the charges against him in accordance with state and federal constitutional due process requirements.

In May 1990, the MQAC filed a motion with the Court of Appeals requesting that they hear the above matter instead of Superior Court. This motion was denied.

The hearing in Superior Court before Judge Terrence Carroll took place August 10, 1990. All of the charges against Warner were dismissed 'without prejudice'. This decision meant that the MQAC could not bring charges against Warner unless they followed their own rules of procedure, which they had not done so far. No longer would the Commission be able to bring vague charges against Warner and compel him to defend himself against unspecified claims. This was a victory of sorts, but it prolonged the agony, continued the legal costs and did not remove the cloud over his head making it impossible for him to hire a doctor to perpetuate his practice as well as continuing the stress and strain of confrontation.

Warner did not hear anything from the MQAC or the Attorney General's office for many months and assumed that perhaps this ordeal was over. Here is a doctor who was supposedly so dangerous to the public that the MQAC waited almost two years (June 1992) to resurrect the same charges and demand that they be answered in twenty days. They gave him three options: a settlement conference (to review the charges), a formal hearing (to refute the charges) or a waiver of both. The third option was tantamount to surrender with the immediate suspension of his license.

Warner chose to have a settlement hearing hoping to come to some mutually acceptable terms with the Commission that would allow him to continue his practice. This hearing was originally scheduled for November 19, 1992 at the SeaTac Motor Inn and was not open to the public. Warner, his lawyer and two witnesses arrived for the 1:00 P.M. meeting only to be told that another hearing was in progress and they would have to wait until 3:00 P.M. Since the principals involved were unable to do that, the hearing was rescheduled for November 30, 1992.

At the subsequent settlement meeting, Dr. Harlow Skinner from Yakima, Washington was in charge of the partial Commission hearing. Warner felt that the meeting was very conciliatory in nature. Those present expressed a desire to help him work out a program to stay in practice until a retirement date of July 1, 1995, when he would be expected to have a new doctor in place to carry on his practice. Some of the conditions suggested were: a periodic review of Warner's patients, rewriting of his patient consent form, informing patients of other options of treatment and requiring them to obtain a second opinion. These conditions were completely acceptable to Warner and he came away from the meeting believing everything was finally settled.

For reasons that were never explained, Warner's lawyer received a call from a Colleen Klein on February 4, 1993 to inform him that the Settlement Hearing conditions were not accepted by the MQAC. Ms Klein said the Commission would reopen the hearing unless Warner agreed to close his practice by July 1, 1993. He never received a letter explaining this complete change in attitude. His lawyer requested minutes of the meeting where the decision not to accept the terms of the Settlement Hearing were made. This request was denied and a formal hearing was scheduled for November 29, 1993. This hearing did not take place and was rescheduled for January 5, 1995, nineteen months after the charges were brought against Warner for the second time.

*   *   *   *

The January 5th hearing began at the Sheraton Tacoma Hotel before Administrative Law Judge (ALJ) James D. Stanford and no members of the MQAC were present. The hearing continued for ten days at this location and was then moved to Seattle at the Bank of California Center on February 3rd, 4th and 7th and concluded after thirteen days of testimony. It should be noted that Warner's patients and supporters filled the hearing room everyday even though the Tacoma location was 50 miles from Seattle.

Thirteen patients testified at the hearing about their cancer experience; what treatment they had received and the quality of their lives under Warner's care. All of these witnesses testified they would have no place to go for their treatment if Warner was denied the right to practice medicine.

There were witnesses on both sides. Four of those testifying against Warner were from the University of Washington——Drs. Robert Jones, Thomas W. Griffin, Robert S. Livingston and Donald Richards.

Two of the witnesses testifying in Warner's behalf were Dr. Lawrence Kiriluk and Dr. Maurice Black from New York.

The charges brought by the MQAC went back to the late 1970s and early 1980s. The Commission had always had the privilege of examining Warner's records at anytime, but since before 1985 had found no cause for censure. During this time, he treated hundreds of patients. Even with all of the negative publicity, his practice continued to grow. He was the only oncologist in the Northwest that I know of who used complementary medicine, a combination of what the Commission calls standard care and other modalities including immunotherapy, diet, vitamins, exercise, attitude and the mind/body connection in healing. So many of the innovative therapies he recommended for many years are now widely accepted.

Six months after the hearing, on July 11, 1994, ALJ James Stanford issued a ninety-three page document titled Findings of Fact, Conclusions of Law and Initial Order. He made the following rulings after careful consideration of all the testimony.

* * * *

PATIENT ONE
  Failure to biopsy—dismissed.
  Wrong diagnosis—dismissed.
  Fine needle aspiration instead of incisional biopsy—sustained.
  Use of immunotherapy—dismissed.
  Failure to recommend hormonal therapy, adjuvant chemotherapy or radiation therapy—dismissed.
  Suggested use of interferon after he was no longer seeing patient. (Chart note, but patient did not return).—dismissed.
  The only charge that was sustained in these charges was the use of two fine needle aspirations of the breast instead of an incisional biopsy. It should be noted that the laboratory results from the fine needle aspirations were negative and that the use of this procedure is standard practice.

* * * *

PATIENT TWO

Failure to recommend surgery instead of radiation therapy—dismissed.

Failure to recommend mastectomy—dismissed.

Failure to recommend to surgeon type of surgery necessary—dismissed.

Radiation treatment of patient—sustained

Failure to document radiation treatment—dismissed

Reliance on the Strelkauskas breast study as a diagnostic tool—dismissed.

All charges dismissed except radiation treatment of this breast cancer patient. This patient was very involved in decisions on her therapy and had consulted with other doctors. She had repeatedly rejected radical surgery and chemotherapy. During the 'expert' testimony there were different opinions on the recommended dosage of radiation. Port films of the patient were inconclusive.

*   *   *   *

PATIENT THREE

Administered radiation in dosage too low to be effective—sustained

Failure to properly inform patient of treatment plan—sustained.

This patient had lung cancer that had spread to regional lymph nodes in 1975. He had surgery, high dose radiation and immunotherapy. He had no further problem until 1984—nine years later. At that time, he had malignant lymphoma and was treated with radiation. The charge was sustained that the dosage used was too high. Also, the charge that the patient was not properly informed of the treatment plan was sustained. This seemed hardly credible to me because I, personally, have never known a doctor who was so patient in his explanations.

*   *   *   *

PATIENT FOUR
    Failure to perform liver test every three months—dismissed.
    Incorrect diagnosis—dismissed.
    Use of immunotherapy in treatment of patient—dismissed.
    Patient diagnosed with leiomyosarcoma in 1986.
    All charges dismissed.

*   *   *   *

PATIENT FIVE
    Failure to arrange for biopsy—dismissed.
    Providing Strelkauskas with small amount of surplus blood—dismissed.
    Failure to recommend adjuvant chemotherapy—dismissed.
    Failure to obtain informed consent for use of BCG—dismissed.
    Patient diagnosed with breast cancer in 1978. She was not seen by
    Dr. Warner until over a year after surgery.
    All charges dismissed.

*   *   *   *

PATIENT SIX
    Failure to adhere to the standard care rule when this patient did not
    choose the most effective course of treatment—dismissed.
    Improper diagnosis—dismissed.
    Patient diagnosed with breast cancer in 1988. She came to Dr.
    Warner for a third opinion after both a surgeon and a radiotherapist
    had recommended an immediate mastectomy. Patient also initially
    rejected his recommendations. It would be difficult to sustain the
    charge of improper diagnosis when the patient had been seen by at
    least two doctors before presenting to Dr. Warner.

*   *   *   *

It seems to me, and probably to the reader, that the charges sustained by Judge Stanford would hardly justify the removal of Glenn Warner's medical license. The practice of medicine is not an exact science and this is particularly true in the treatment of cancer. There are widely differing opinions among practicing oncologists. In the Initial Order, Stanford ordered that Glenn A. Warner be issued a reprimand for the violations that were upheld. That he "shall be restricted by the disciplinary authority in that he shall no longer practice radiological therapy until he demonstrates to the said disciplinary authority that he has sufficient skills to perform this form of therapy, shall be imposed a fine of $6,000, and shall be suspended for a term of ninety days with ten days presently imposed. The imposing of the eighty day balance of the suspension term shall be deferred for a period of three years on the condition that the Respondent conduct his practice at or above the standard of care at all times."

It should be noted here that Warner had not practiced radiation therapy for many years and had no intention of doing so in the future. Although Judge Stanford's Findings and Conclusions were not completely what Warner had hoped for, it was a conclusion he could live with and still take care of his patients. Of primary importance is the fact that Judge Stanford did not recommend revoking his license.

CHAPTER 7

THE INQUISITION CONTINUES

Although there were no charges against Warner for the kind of treatment he recommended for his patients, that issue came up over and over as Beverly Goetz, the attorney representing the Attorney General's office, hammered at witnesses about what constituted informed consent and what was standard care. All of the prosecutor's witnesses testified many times during the thirteen day hearing that the only acceptable care for cancer patients is surgery, radiation and chemotherapy.

In my opinion, this should have been reason enough to overturn the whole proceedings because we have a law in the State of Washington, House Bill 1960, RCW 18.130 180 effective May 21, 1991, which states: "The use of nontraditional treatment by itself shall not constitute unprofessional conduct, provided that it does not result in injury to a patient or create an unreasonable risk that a patient may be harmed."

With Stanford's decision, is this ordeal finally over? No, it is not. On August 2, 1994, the MQAC, upon the advice of the Assistant Attorney General, Beverly Goetz, did not accept Judge Stanford's Findings & Conclusions. It should be noted here that in spite of thirteen days of testimony, the expense of such a hearing and the time involved, the MQAC is not required to accept the Findings & Conclusions of the presiding judge. This is wrong! If the Commission appoints an ALJ to preside at a disciplinary hearing and requires the defendant to be present or surrender his license, it should be required to accept the decision of that judge.

Eventually, I made an effort to determine how and who made the decision not to accept Judge Stanford's Findings of Fact & Conclusions of Law in regard to the thirteen day hearing. On October 13, 1997, I wrote the MQAC and, under the Freedom of Information Act, requested copies of its minutes of meetings where the charges against Dr. Glenn Warner were discussed. I specifically asked for copies of minutes where the decision was made not to accept Judge Stanford's decision and to petition for review. Such a meeting should have taken place between August 2, 1994 and February 24, 1995.

On October 22, 1997, I received a letter from Mike Kramer, Public Disclosure Coordinator for the MQAC, saying such information would be provided in approximately three weeks.

Sometime later I called Mike Kramer to check on the progress of my request and he referred me to Lisa Pigott, Administrative Assistant. She told me I would have to buy transcripts of the minutes from Lewis & Associates. I contacted them and they could not locate the information I requested.

After several telephone conversations, Lisa Pigott told me that in pursuing my request she had found that there were no minutes kept of any meetings regarding charges against Warner and the decisions that were made regarding the disposition of this case. This was on December 9, 1997 and I immediately wrote her the following letter.

*   *   *   *

"Dear Lisa:

"Relevant to our conversation this morning, I am requesting you verify in writing what you told me on the phone.

Specifically, that the MQAC held meetings or telephone conversations on actions that affected a doctor's livelihood and the welfare of his patients without recording any of their conversations or decisions.

In other words, there are no records of whether they did or did not have meetings. I find it impossible to believe that any State Commission can have secret, unrecorded meetings with no accountability to the public.

Thank you for your help."

I received the following letter in reply dated December 22, 1997.

*   *   *   *

"Dear Ms Berry:

"This letter is in response to your letter dated December 9, 1997 in which you requested that I verify in writing our conversation of earlier this week. This also responds to an earlier letter written by you on October 13, 1997, which precipitated the previously mentioned telephone conversations.

"Per established procedure, as administered by the Office of Professional Standards, there were meetings held in closed session, either in person or telephonically, with Administrative Law Judge Brian Peyton. As I stated to you in our conversations, there were no court reporter or staff members present at those discussions. As an analogy it might help to think of the Commission members as jurors in a civil trial. While the trial itself is open to the public, the jury goes into closed session to deliberate on the case and to reach judgment or verdict.

"The department filed a petition for review and the Commission members along with Brian Peyton as their legal advisor, decided to honor the petition. As a further point of clarification, it is the prosecuting Assistant Attorney General who decided to issue a petition for review, or in circumstances unfavorable to the respondent, the physicians counsel will file the petition hoping for hearing resulting in a different decision more favorable to their client. Please be assured that the petition was not filed by the Commission members making the decision whether or not to hear the petition. (My underline).

"You also asked that I provide you with a date for public disclosure of any of the above-mentioned proceedings. The only portion that was recorded would have been the actual hearing on the petition for review which was held on February 24, 1997. (Wrong date-L.B.). As previously mentioned you will need to contact Robert Lewis and Associates at (253) 952-2030 and ask for a copy of that transcript.

"I hope this information is of assistance and shed some light on the process of administrative law. I can be reached at (360) 664-2578 with any further questions.

"Respectfully, (Signed) Lisa Pigott, Administrative Assistant".

I think it is of particular interest that Lisa Pigott likens the Commission to a jury. No members of the Commission attended the thirteen day hearing before Judge Stanford so how could they be qualified to act as a jury? Also, the letter states that the Assistant Attorney General, as prosecutor, made the decision, not the Commission members. Now that's bizarre! The prosecutor did not get the results she wanted at the thirteen day hearing, namely the revocation of Glenn Warner's license, so, according to this letter from the Department of Health, she can petition for review and then is the person who accepts her petition.

*   *   *   *

Over six months later on February 24, 1995, a petition for review was heard by ALJ Brian Peyton and doctors Stan Tuell, retired general surgeon from Tacoma, Washington, M. Estelle Connolly, head and neck plastic surgeon from Tacoma, Washington, William Marineau, retired family practitioner from Spokane, Washington and David Williams, doctor of internal medicine from Yakima, Washington. The doctors were all members of the MQAC. This was a short hearing with lawyers from both sides given very limited time to present their arguments. I was present at this hearing and would like to know if the Judge and four doctors sitting in judgment had read the 1,500 pages of testimony of the hearing before Judge Stanford. Or, were they basing their decision on the abbreviated arguments of the petition for review and the opinion of the prosecuting attorney?

Until July 18, 1995, almost five months from the hearing, there had been no communication from the MQAC or Attorney General's office by phone or letter to Warner or his lawyers. Then, on this date, with no warning, three individuals representing the MQAC came into his office and demanded that he surrender his license immediately. Needless to say, Warner did not accommodate them.

On August 10, 1995, there was a hearing in Superior Court before Judge Michael Hayden asking for an injunction to stay the revocation of Warner's license until such time as this matter could be fully heard in Superior Court. As usual, the courtroom was full of Warner's supporters and dozens more waited in the hallway. Judge Hayden heard the arguments, recessed for fifteen minutes, came back to the courtroom and granted the injunction.

The full hearing was scheduled for February 26, 1996, subsequently changed to February 27th in Superior Court. On February 20th, at the last possible moment, Judge Hayden withdrew from the case citing a conflict of interest. This has always seemed strange to me since he had six months from the hearing on the injunction to figure this out. Why didn't he recuse himself earlier? The hearing was then assigned to a Judge Doty and rescheduled for March 14, 1996. This hearing did not take place.

On March 15, 1996, the hearing was assigned to Judge Robert Lasnik and scheduled for March 19th. Four days seems very little time to prepare for a case of this magnitude with hundred of pages of documents to be read in order to have an understanding of the issues. However, the hearing did take place and Judge Lasnik said he hoped to have a decision by April 4, 1996.

There was no communication from the Court or the MQAC until June 14, 1996 when Warner was notified that Lasnik had upheld the revocation of his license effective immediately.

*   *   *   *

This decision amply demonstrated that the Commission is all powerful. In his decision, Judge Lasnik made several statements that support this conclusion. He wrote, "Some of Dr. Warner's theories about cancer treatments are controversial in the medical profession. He and his supporters, who credit Dr. Warner with heroic and effective care and treatment of themselves and their loved ones, claim the medical orthodoxy has singled Dr. Warner out for special punishment because of his use of alternative treatments. The Commission has denied that its actions were motivated in any way by Dr. Warner's use of non-traditional treatment except where it resulted in injury to the patient or created an unreasonable risk of harm to the patient."

"This is 'deferential' review standard where the court is prohibited from substituting its judgment for that of the agency. Dr. Warner has pointed out that the findings of the ALJ (Administrative Law Judge) were modified by the Commission and that this court should restore the findings and conclusions in the Initial Order over those in the Final Order. However, the Attorney General correctly points out that under RCW 34.05.464 the Commission was entitled to substitute its own findings for those made by the hearing officer, and those findings as modified or replaced by the Commission, are the ones which are relevant to Superior Court." (My underline)

"While Dr. Warner has presented another perspective on the facts of these five cases, the Commission was entitled to exercise its perogative as fact finder not to afford credence to the opinions of Dr. Warner or his witnesses.

"The final decision for this court—and one which has caused the court considerable consternation—is the determination of what sanction should Dr.Warner suffer for these transgressions....In fact, this court disagrees with the Commission and would fashion a different sanction. This court would allow Dr. Warner to continue his practice in restricted areas with oversight and with full disclosure to his patients....It seems especially hard to punish indirectly some of Dr. Warner's current patients who will have their course of treatment interrupted. But this court's disagreement with the sanction imposed by the Commission is not a basis to find that the punishment is 'arbitrary and capricious'.

"We cannot substitute our judgment for that of the board, even if we were to see the evidence differently from the agency."

It was obvious from Judge Lasnik's decision that there was not much point in asking the Superior Court to hear this case, but it was decided to make one more effort. On June 28, 1996, Commissioner William Ellis of the Court of Appeals heard a motion asking for a stay of Judge Lasnik's decision until the matter could be heard by the full Court of Appeals. On July 2, 1996, the motion was denied.

*   *   *   *

A motion was filed for a hearing before the full Court of Appeals. This motion was later withdrawn when it was decided that it was futile to go on. It had been made abundantly clear that the State Commission had made its decision and there was nothing that could be done to change it. If the MQAC had told Warner and his legal counsel in the beginning that no matter what he did, what arguments were presented or what his patients said about his care, it would have no bearing on their decision perhaps it could have saved time, money and emotional distress.

It is beyond my belief that it is possible that an agency, which is supposed to serve the citizens of this State, could be so all-powerful. In fact, it is frightening!

This lengthy persecution of one doctor alerted citizen groups who have tried to get changes made through the State Legislature. They have written letters, traveled to the State Capitol in Olympia, Washington to attend hearings and talked to their representatives all to no avail. They promise to keep trying. The changes requested that would affect the MQAC seem very reasonable.

1. The MQAC consists of nineteen members. At the present time, three members can decide to revoke a doctor's license. The citizen's groups have requested this be changed to a majority of the members.

The language to accomplish this was originally in House Bill 2188. The sponsors of this legislation agreed that for a matter so serious as taking away a physician's livelihood and denying his patients his care that it should require a vote of a majority of the MQAC. This part of the bill was deleted before it came to a vote at the request of the MQAC.

2. That an Administrative Law Judge always hear disciplinary actions against any doctor and that the MQAC be required to accept the ALJ's findings and conclusions. The MQAC who brings the charges against a doctor are already prejudiced and the ALJ brings an unbiased, impartial presence to the proceedings.

3. A statute of limitations on actions by the MQAC. A time period of three years from the time charges are brought to a resolution or the charges will be dropped.

One change in the procedure of the MQAC was made several years ago. Until then, physicians appointed themselves to the Commission. This was changed by the legislature to make the Governor responsible for appointments. The citizen's group that worked for this change was hopeful that it would result in a Commission that was more representative and understanding of alternative and complementary medicine. However, not one physician or lay person they have recommended has ever been appointed by the Governor to the MQAC.

I arranged a meeting with then Governor Lowry as a last ditch effort to reverse the decision by the MQAC. This took place on October 24, 1996. Glenn and Helen Warner and several cancer patients attended this meeting with me. The Governor's legal counsel, Kent Caputo, was also in attendance. Both Lowry and Caputo were sympathetic but said the Governor had no authority to overturn a decision by the Commission. Interestingly enough, the Governor does have the power to overturn the courts; such as, pardoning a criminal. The meeting was pleasant but nothing was accomplished. Both the Governor and his lawyer suggested that changes need to be made through the legislature to make the MQAC less autonomous and more responsive to the will of the citizens of the state. The changes suggested above, if they are ever implemented, will not help Warner, but they might help other doctors in the future who find themselves in the same situation.

PART III

PHILOSOPHY DIAGNOSIS AND TREATMENT

SUCCESS STORIES

CHAPTER 8

DR. WARNER'S PHILOSOPHY

Over the years of medical training, study, research work and patient care, Warner developed a philosophy different from the approach used by other oncologists in the Seattle area. His approach to cancer therapy developed evolving over many years because of the failures of standard treatment (radiation and chemotherapy) that he witnessed and a desire to find a more effective and humane way to treat patients. Quality of life while undergoing treatment was also of paramount consideration of this doctor.

During an interview, Dr. Warner expressed the following thoughts on his philosophy.

He believed it was the attitude of the patient about his disease that, to a great extent, influenced the course of his illness, response to therapy, and the healing qualities that would be the result of whatever treatments were given. He felt that there were so many parts to this illness that it was necessary to use every approach possible to confront it.

He stated that we need to use Western medicine with its high technology. However, he believed Western technology had gone off on a tangent and forgotten the patient so that many doctors no longer knew how to care for people. He believed that doctors should go back to the Eastern approach to medicine which is caring for the individual more than working on the disease. He thought many Eastern programs were successful because they made the patient stronger. He found that if patients had the right attitude and corrected certain things their disease would be kept under control for a prolonged period of time. Because it was not destructive, it was going to be better than what is done in very aggressive and invasive Western medicine.

Cancer is not a crisis situation. It is the result of a chronic illness that occurs over time. It is the summation of tiny injuries and scars that accumulate. Finally, the cells that try to replace the defect are asked to do so rapidly and they are often immature. These cells are not able to function as well as mature cells. These immature cells begin to affect the blood flow and the lymphatic flow. Circulation begins to break down. The patient begins to accumulate toxins. If the body, through diet and lifestyle, is not ingesting the right kind of material, these toxins build up at a more rapid pace. This creates a strongly stimulating environment that causes these abnormal cells to grow more rapidly and they are not turned off by the normal mechanism which usually tells the cells when to stop.

As a result of this, we get the overgrowth of these very immature cells that do not function properly. This obstructs and squeezes out the function in that particular region as a rule, which results in the symptoms that take us to the doctor. The pain of the swelling, the obstruction that occurs in the mass that develops, the sore that does not heal, the bleeding, and so on. These are the cardinal effects of a symptomatic malignancy, the functional stage of this process, and to put all of our emphasis on the symptoms and not try to understand what produces those effects will doom us to failure.

This is what has happened to Western medicine now. Many have given up caring for the patient in the belief that the physician can, through high tech approaches, get rid of the cells or make a change that would cause the process to stop on its own. However, the feeder lines usually continue and from various directions this process smolders on. As long as there is one cell remaining, it is only a matter of time until that cell will come back and grow to the same size as the original, causing problems that have to be dealt with.

The doctor who says, "Come back and see me in six months or a year or whenever you have symptoms is missing a golden opportunity". The doctor should be setting up a maintenance program that will prevent that patient from producing the tumor again. It is this approach that makes it possible to think of controlling cancer. Medical science probably never will get to the point of curing cancer although, through genetic engineering, individual tumors may be eliminated.

It comes back to a combination of treatments and a combination of caring people who contribute to this process. The patient, first of all, has to change his diet and lifestyle around, making the body receptive to the healing process. This will take away the wastes and toxins that are in the body. These have built up because of inadequate metabolism at the tumor site, which serve as stimulating factors to make these abnormal cells grow.

Recent work in genetic engineering has shown that, by manipulation, normal cells assume malignant characteristics. Malignant cells can be stimulated genetically so they revert to normal. This work indicates that this is not a static process. It is a process that can be manipulated and it is not inevitable that the patient is going to succumb to his disease. There is never a situation where there is not something the doctor can do. Whether enough is done is critical.

There are some misconceptions about immunotherapy. Many people talk about it and there are a lot of people pushing vitamin and herbal products that do not have any true value as far as immunity is concerned. Promoters of these products say that they stimulate the immune system without always knowing what makes it function.

        *   *   *   *

Immunity is the body's ability to respond to injury. There are many ways this can be accomplished, but it all comes from within the individual. The individual's body, metabolically and physiologically, undergoes changes that makes it able to heal itself. Because the body's inherent mechanisms are there for healing and not for producing something abnormal or bad, it is also there to correct any of these bad changes that may occur to the detriment of the individual. So the individual has this mechanism working for him and, as we learn more about it, we know that it is far more complex and involves many different areas of the body.

That is why Warner concentrated more on biologic therapy—the theory that life-giving matters are more important as far as treatments are concerned for whatever disease in which the immune mechanisms are engaged. In cancer, it is really a failure of the immune system that allows the process to get started and to continue to grow because the body is supposed to recognize these abnormal mutant cells that develop as a result of DNA damage and correct them. Failure to get rid of the abnormal cells allows the process to go on until it can get to the point of overwhelming the defense mechanisms. In immunotherapy, the body needs to be stimulated in such a way that it makes more of these immune factors come into play and, as a result, helps the body control these abnormal growth patterns.

It begins with simple things. The patient must exercise and rehabilitate his body to the point that it begins to function efficiently. The patient must realize that it demands real change and most people pay lip service to change. Apparently, some people can get by with certain things and the tumor will not be stimulated to grow. These factors are not known and the patient cannot take that chance. It has to be a wholehearted commitment on the part of the patient to do everything he/she can do to make the body work more efficiently.

This did not mean just the physical aspect. It means the mind/body relationship as well. It is a commitment that takes time and organization to do properly. There are things that need to be corrected and if this is accomplished, the tumor problem has a much better chance of coming under control. In other words, a tumor will not grow in an environment that is healthy and healing and repairing.

This whole process depends on the stage of the illness. It may be a stage of so-called insitu lesion, which is confined to just one area. It will probably develop into an invasive tumor, but it has not as yet invaded other areas. This situation can be dealt with surgically and the cancerous cells removed, but the process that caused those cells to form will be continuing to act. Just because you have removed the major portion of the tumor that was present does not mean that you are not going to have additional cells continue to grow and come back again. It does make good sense that in addition to medical intervention, Warner's patients were asked to do everything possible to reduce the tumor volume and the environment that caused the cancer.

Consider how many cancers could be eliminated by changing a few things. It is accepted that environmental factors contribute to cancer. There are job associated illnesses that cause cancer—asbestosis leading to respiratory diseases and individuals who make tires have bladder cancer because of the solvents that are necessary in making the synthetic rubber. There are certain parasites that get into the body that, in some situations, will produce cancer. There are so many external things that can get into the body and cause tumor. By eliminating cancer causing environmental factors, the immune system is strengthened.

  *   *   *   *

The immune system, most of the time, is triggered into action by the white cells. These cells have the capacity to act as alarmists and to alert the body's defense mechanisms that there is an intruder aboard. Something must be done to stimulate the immune system. In the first phase of immunotherapy, the first step is to increase the white cells. There are vaccines of a non-specific nature that will stimulate the immune system to make antibodies against a particular bacterial product. The good of this approach is that in stimulating the defense mechanism, the whole immune system acts as an orchestra in concert. Therefore, the immunity against the agent injected is strengthened in addition to other ancillary, or associated, secondary associations, that might be against tumors and allergic manifestations. It is not a specific thing just for that particular material in the vaccine, but it makes all of the immune system respond. Indirectly, there will be more cells that will be stimulated. The non-specific immune stimulation is extremely important.

The vaccines can be bacterial vaccines such as BCG (Bacillus Calmette Guerin). There are certain staphochocal products or the parts of staphochocal organisms that can be used that will stimulate various parts of the immune system. Interferon is a product that is given off by the white cells which recruits new white cells into the area. They secrete materials that stimulate the next phase in the healing process or they may be directly cytotoxic against the tumor itself. This is why it is essential to get the white cells going and it is known that even though they may not be directly related to the immune system, all of the white cells will contribute in some manner to the immune protection.

Sometimes the demand for control of the disease needs more than just white cells. It is necessary to reduce the volume of tumor. In order to do that, the procedure that is of the most value and probably is the most specific therapy of an invasive nature that will be helpful is surgery. Of all the so-called conventional therapies that are used, surgery is the only one that has any significant influence. There are a few times that radiation therapy and chemotherapy have demonstrated that they have an effect that justifies their use, but most of the time the destructive effects outweigh the advantages of using these modalities.

Since it is known the tumor has been growing for years prior to the symptomatic stage when the surgeon first sees the lump or the obstruction, it is an accepted fact that the tumor has been circulating throughout the body for years before it even gets to this stage. Taking out the primary lesion does not always get rid of all the tumor cells that have been circulating in the blood lymphatic system for many years and which the body has been keeping under control. The body has made antibodies and other biologic materials against that particular tumor and has been able to generally keep it under control. But, eventually, it may have progressed to a point where it is not able to do so because the volume of tumor is such that the body's immune system cannot keep up with it. The surgeon removes the tumor mass and what is left plus the immunity the patient has developed against the tumor may be enough to irradicate anymore problems. The surgeon removes what he can see and often that is not enough. A report from the pathologist is necessary after surgery to make sure there isn't some cancer the surgeon missed.

When the majority of the tumor is removed, the patient's own immune system is a little bit stronger. With the reduction of the tumor mass, the immune system can rally. It is even possible that the immune system will be strong enough to control the problem without the patient having any other aggressive or harmful therapy. If a maintenance program is not begun to help the immune system recover from the trauma of surgery, the cancer will often come back in a short period of time depending upon the growth rate of the tumor cell itself.

*   *   *   *

Tumor markers are used to determine if the tumor has been completely removed. These are tumor associated antigens that arise on the surface of the tumor cell that are somewhat specific for that tumor and are fairly universal regardless of the individual. They are an indicator of the presence of tumor, of its disappearance indicating a favorable response to therapy or a rising level indicating further growth. When the tumor is surgically removed, the tumor marker should drop to a very low level or disappear. There are antigens present in the blood stream and by special techniques the laboratory can tell how much of this tumor antigen is circulating in the bloodstream. If most of the tumor is removed, this antigen should disappear. Tumor markers are used periodically and if the doctor continues to watch and the tumor starts back again, the tumor marker starts to rise indicating that the patient is getting into trouble and needs maintenance with more specific therapy.

The doctor needs to be aware that the tumor marker may indicate an impending problem and still be within normal range. In other words, if the tumor marker level is 1, the next time the reading is 2, the next time it is 3 or 4 even though the normal is up to 10, the fact that it is slowly increasing should alert the doctor to the fact that there is probably going to be a relapse in that tumor situation. Then specific things should be done that will initiate a correction. It may be that the patient is not giving up his old bad habits and the doctor will have to tell him that a low fat—low sugar diet and exercise are important in the process of healing. The patient has to build up his body so the mechanisms used to defend itself are brought back into play in a way that can help in the healing process.

The tumor markers become an extremely important way of following the patient's progress. The number of tumor markers available is rising all the time. There are hundreds of tumor markers being investigated in research areas that could be of use now. If doctors were allowed to use them, we could see what value they are to the patient. They are restricted because they are not specific, but that is not their purpose. The rise or fall of tumor markers may or may not mean the presence of some inflammatory reaction. It could be a normal reaction. Exercise, stress or anxiety will make the white counts go up or down. Everything is a rhythmical or cyclical change so an exact measurement is not possible.

*   *   *   *

There are patients who do very well for a period of time then, suddenly, everything falls apart. What happens? First of all, it was Warner's experience that many of these people who are seemingly doing very well and following everything to the letter are not. In their minds, they are doing what they think should be done, but they don't realize the degree of commitment they have to make in order to make themselves well. The DNA is very sensitive to changes that occur, and it doesn't take much to produce a profound change if you bathe them with toxic materials. Perhaps some patients follow a regimen very carefully in the beginning stages of their disease, but then they become lax. The very common thing with all of us is that when the initial problem is brought under control we go back to our old comfortable lifestyle. It has to do with our subconscious mind and the way we react to situations. We feel more comfortable when we are not challenging or trying to change or do something different. When we begin to do the things that make our body change the way it reacts, our body labors in this change of habit.

Learning to deal with stress has much to do with our physical well being. This is extremely important and, usually, stress is of our own making. In other words, some stress is necessary to grow and learn. If the stress becomes painful producing dysfunction with it, it becomes harmful. Life is a series of stressful events that change in degree of intensity all the time. The degree of intensity also changes with our perceptions. If you are a person who wants to be in full control of everything, then that stress is going to be very harmful. Often things do not work out the way we desire as much as we try.

Because of negative thinking, the brain cells secrete chemical substances called neurotransmitters. These react with hormonal systems, the immune system or the nervous system to produce a dysfunctional reaction. Stress may stimulate certain kinds of hormone or growth factors that will stimulate the tumor to grow. Or, it will deny substances the body puts into that tumor to destroy it. It also could constrict the blood flow or the lymphatic flow into the area so those things the body normally produces to kill a tumor are not allowed into it. Life without stress is impossible and it is important. It is the driving force that helps us to accommodate to where and who we are. It is our reaction to stress that will determine whether it is going to be good stress or bad stress.

An important factor in managing stress is not getting stressed out over things you cannot control. Some people have real tragedy in their lives such as losing a child or a spouse. Everybody grieves differently, of course, but those stressful situations often make people ill. Some individuals dwell on their tragic situations to the point that they literally make themselves sick. This is often seen in cancer situations where the remaining spouse comes down with an illness within a year that results in death. You have to let go of being in control and let God. You do that in whatever context you have a spiritual life.

If the volume of tumor is not reduced, the immune system will not be strong enough. The same thing is true with depression and unless the doctor helps the person overcome, the patient cannot make positive steps. That is why it is so important that the physician discusses diet, lifestyle, exercise, meditation, imagery and healing relationships in the very beginning of his relationship with the patient. If the patient changes, his body is going to be stronger and more reactive against the tumor. The more you do to strengthen your body, the more effective your therapy will be whether it is surgery, radiation or chemotherapy. It is known that the person who has radiation treatment has less nausea and vomiting if he is properly prepared mentally. The same is true with chemotherapy. It has been demonstrated with many patients that the more these people are supported, the more likely the patient's loss of hair will be kept to a minimum. There will not be as many depressions of the blood forming mechanisms that are essential for immune reactivity—the white cells specifically—and the patient will not be as sick.

*　　　*　　　*　　　*

Warner said that he could tell on the first visit whether the patient was a person who was willing to take charge and cooperate in the healing process. Patients often complain that the doctor does not listen. Sometimes the situation is the opposite—the patients often did not listen to what he was trying to tell them. They had a preconceived idea that unless they received surgery, radiation or chemotherapy, they were not going to get well. He tried to tell the patient that this was not the most important part.

Those therapies are often essential in the treatment program to reduce the size of the volume of the tumor, but that is just the first big step to get the patient started on the road to healing. If maintenance therapy is not done, and if an effort is not made to correct the things that started the process in the first place, there will be failure. There is no reason to be doing all the initial treatments if the patient will not make lifestyle changes. If the patient wants to improve his health, if he wants to take charge, if he wants to live, if life is worthwhile, if he has a mission in life he wants to fulfill, then that demands that he does something about it.

Conventional therapies are important and often very necessary, but they really should be complementary to the other kinds of treatment used. They should not be the dominant approach as they are used now except for surgical intervention. Surgery gets rid of as much of the tumor as possible, tells us the kind of tumor, what that tumor is doing to our body, and what the body is doing against the tumor. There are signs and symptoms in the body that can be determined by surgical exploration that will aid the doctor in the treatment program.

Radiation therapy can reduce volume of tumor, but the amount of damage it does to normal tissues may be far greater than the good it can do. There are areas where the tumor is not a surgically treatable situation. Then the x-ray therapy will be a form of surgical removal. It is less effective in getting rid of tumors and the non-specific effect of chemotherapy agents limits their value. Until a way is found to take those chemical agents inside the cell without spilling out into normal tissue and confine the damage by these agents, they are not going to be effective except in stopping the abnormal, very rapid growth of some tumors in which the cells multiply so rapidly that there is no other way to get at them. These are the leukemias, some lymphomas and some of the germ cell tumors. In some situations, using these agents to rapidly reduce the volume of tumor enables the body's immune system to take over, and the patient will gain control. However, this is less then 5% of all the cancers we face.

Physicians are limited by their technological approach because they are trying to use external influences to treat an internally caused disease. Unless the patient is directly involved in the decision making process and biologic mechanisms are used as the main form of therapy, the possibility of long term control will not going to be very good.

*   *   *   *

Another important aspect of the patient's journey toward wellness is a support group. One of Warner's patients started such a group in 1985 at a church in Bellevue, Washington (a suburb outside of Seattle). It meets every Wednesday night the year around. Every week 35 to 50 cancer patients and their families gather to share their fears and hopes.

Glenn Warner and his wife, Helen, always attended all of these meetings. He listened and talked for about ten minutes at the end always offering hope and encouragement. I don't know of another doctor who would have devoted this much time to an informal talk group. I asked him why he did it and he said, "I learn more about my patients here then I ever do on an office visit and that insight helps me to help them."

Longtime survivors attend to share their experience with the new patients who are in the initial stage of treatment. They set an example of what is possible. The group is uplifting because of the sharing of a devastating disease and the combined efforts to beat it and emerge a better person. Many survivors, including myself, have said that cancer enriched their lives. How could that possibly be true? Because the diagnosis of a life-threatening disease caused them to examine every aspect of their lives and make changes for the better.

CHAPTER 9

The following eight chapters discussing different types of diagnosis and treatment of cancer and general comments are the result of interviews by Richard Stannard with Glenn Warner, transcribed and edited to their present form.

BREAST CANCER

It is not possible to be specific about the treatments used for various phases of breast cancer. There are some generalities but the specifics must be determined by direct intervention of an oncologist who, along with the patient, maps out a program that will be suitable. As in any other disease, unless the patient is cooperative and believes in the treatment and has faith in the practitioner's ability to deliver the treatment, there is not going to be a successful conclusion. The major problem with breast cancer is that we are looking at it as if it is a catastrophic illness affecting women and that it is different then any other disease situation.

Often women have fibrocystic disease of the breast. There are hormone changes and irregularities in the growth pattern. The body destroys and reconstructs some of the finer architecture in the breast on a monthly basis with each menstrual cycle. This then leads to the development of too much growth in the lining of the milk ducts in the breast, which can produce obstructions if the excess cellular content is not removed, and the drainage reestablished. It can then go on to form cysts. These can be quite irritating and produce changes in the duct itself or the structures around the duct and, as such, make nodules. The nodules, or lumps, then become a concern because they could portend the development of malignancy. As these develop, the need to find out what is there is accentuated by the woman's belief that a breast tumor is an aggressive, irreconcilable disease that will rapidly kill her. So early attempts are made to diagnose. Fibrocystic disease is not cancer. It is a benign disease of the breast. However, because of this concern, some women have multiple breast biopsies and many of the lumps removed are benign. In fact, some studies show that as high as 70% of the lumps removed are benign. Therefore, you then make the patient cancer conscious through this process.

This cancer consciousness and the fear of death keep a patient always on edge. There is a lack of harmony in the mind/body relationship because of this concern. Now there may be something in the mind/body relationship that does, through endocrine stimulation, enhance or increase the speed with which the fibrocystic disease may develop or change. It may be irritating to preexisting breast changes.

All of this gives a very disquieting pattern to the patient's approach to the breast, oftentimes to her relationship with her husband and other psychological changes, which make this an ongoing problem. The more depressed, fearful and anxious the patient becomes, the more imunosuppression may develop. This results in the inability of the patient's natural surveillance system to change the irregular growth pattern in the breast back to normal so the disease can be brought under control and remain a benign fibrocystic disease.

Some of the unnecessary concern about breast cancer is driven by economics. Constant warnings to women to self-exam their breasts and to have regular breast examinations can be counter productive and sometimes harmful. A prime example is the use of the mammography. Increasingly, women are directed to start having mammograms fairly early in life. Some say you should have your first mammogram at least by age 35.

Dr. Gofman at the University of California has reported that the exposure to radiation for medical purposes has increased and may be the cause of over three-quarters of the breast cancers that develop. So, in effect, with diagnostic mammography trying to get an early diagnosis it may be producing the very problem we are trying to eliminate. Dr. Gofman is a learned and knowledgeable investigator and has the facts and figures to back up what he is saying, but it certainly is not having any influence on the continued advertising that is being done to get women in for early mammography.

*   *   *   *

The patient needs to have early diagnosis, but it is not absolutely necessary to do the x-ray version such as a mammography. Ultra sound uses sound waves and is not radioactive. New machines used in ultra sound are becoming much better in defining the structures in the breast that allow the doctor to be aware of nodules when they are big enough to be significant. Then the doctor would not be caught in the dilemma of trying to decide if these very tiny nodules that were seen on mammogram are due to malignancy or just the normal change in breast physiology.

After the ultra sound, the doctor can decide whether there is a need for further study. Magnetic Resonance Imaging (MRI) can be used which, again, is not radiation. Magnetic studies can be done that are probably more definitive then the mammogram. An MRI gives more information about the condition in the breasts, the regional lymph nodes, and the chest lymph nodes. It is a much better way of getting more information which will be helpful in deciding whether the patient has a localized or systemic disease both of which would be treated entirely differently.

Once it is determined that a woman does have breast cancer, a decision must be made as to the treatment options. It must be treated because the mass will continue to grow. If it is not treated early, it starts spreading to other parts of the body going, usually, first to the lymph nodes under the arm although it can bypass that and go directly into the blood stream or into the bone. The disease then becomes very difficult to treat because we have nothing that will go specifically to breast tumor cells and kill them. There are the cyto-toxic chemotherapy drugs that go to any cell that is dividing and destroy the reproductive mechanism so they will not continue living. However, these drugs do not distinguish between normal and abnormal tissues. In certain situations, the damage will be greater in normal tissues, specifically the immune system, then they would be to the tumor.

*   *   *   *

There is a drug called tamoxifen, but before using tamoxifen the doctor needs to know first of all if there a malignancy and what that malignancy is doing. Is it a malignancy that may be dormant? Nodules can be removed and if the disease measures less then two centimeters and there is no spread to other tissues and has good margins around the breast nodules it can be left alone. Good margins means surrounding tissue are free from invasion by tumor from the primary source. Tumor spreads much like the roots of a tree and the surgeon needs to make sure he gets all around that so-called root ball that designates the extension of the tumor. Almost 90% of people in this category will go 5 to 10 years before there is any evidence of any local recurrence. It would be very rare for it to be systemic.

The reason for treatment, of course, is if these cells are not kept under control, they will eventually invade other parts of the body. Some parts, when invaded, will lead to failure of the organism to live for one reason or another. So the main thing is to begin the treatment at the earliest possible time. The patient needs to make sure that the disease cannot be controlled by lesser means other than some of the aggressive treatments that are currently used and are more harmful to the patient. This would include doing mastectomies when a lumpectomy would be sufficient. Warner did not recommend disfiguring procedures when the breasts could be preserved. Then the patient would not be harmed by psychological damage from the amount of disfigurement that resulted.

Warner used a different approach for breast cancer with BCG and other immune therapies. These were part of the integrative approach. In other words, using any method that had shown some value and no harm should be incorporated in the treatment program. This is the secret of the success he had because he used a large number of agents that had shown value in other tumors. When these were applied to individual patients, he was gratified to see an excellent response, oftentimes in cases that he did not fully understand in the beginning.

BCG is Bacillus Calmette-Guerin, named after the two Frenchmen who discovered the bacteria that causes tuberculosis in cattle. When the use of BCG was first begun by the National Cancer Institute, it was used to treat a cancer in the eye of cattle. The localized tumor was much like cancer of the breast except it was located in the orbit area. The BCG was injected directly into that area with almost miraculous results in the large number of animals they were able to treat. Dr. Herbert Raap, an immunologist with the National Cancer Institute, was one of the leading investigators of this and then tried to see if this could apply to the human situation. This necessitated going through the laborious task of converting this kind of information to usage in human tumors and it took a great deal of work. Local injections were used most of the time for determining its value and treatment.

There were studies that augmented this in a different way. In those parts of the world where BCG was used as a vaccination for children to prevent tuberculosis, it was noted that those children that had the BCG inoculations had lower incidences of malignancies. Dr. Mathe in France then used that as a means of maintaining the resolution of leukemia that he was getting in some patients with high dose chemotherapy. Survivors of this program led to the use of BCG in this country. It was tried in many different ways and it was never very successful as a permanent treatment until practitioners began to look back at the successes and found out that whenever BCG was injected as close to the tumor as possible, it was more effective.

At one time, there were many major medical schools throughout the United States trying to find the reason for the improvement in survival when the vaccine was injected directly into the lesion. Because there was some contaminated BCG vaccine, several children died. That led to the Americans rejecting the use of BCG as a childhood vaccination. For that reason, there was no information on long-term use of BCG.

Warner became involved in the use of BCG on a research program with melanoma. He, personally, felt if it would work in melanoma, it should be tried on a wide variety of tumors to see whether it would be beneficial. He was stimulating the immune system and later found that it raised the level of interferon, a hormone substance secreted by the patient's lymphocytes, which helps control the abnormal cells that are developing in all of us all the time. BCG has no specific effect for individual tumors. It's specific effect on immune enhancement and modulation is what leads to its continued use today in many research projects that are still being conducted by major universities.

At the present time, the Federal Drug Administration (FDA) approves BCG for only one phase of bladder cancer. Warner used it in any tumor situation, including breast cancer, in which he felt the patient was immuno suppressed and he needed to enhance immune reaction against the tumor.

*   *   *   *

As an example, there was one particular case of breast cancer where BCG was used very successfully. Peggy (name changed) had a tumor that had spread to 18 axillary lymph nodes. She had surgery to remove the tumor and what is called an axillary clean out. In other words, the surgeon removed as many of the lymph nodes as possible. Her prognosis was not good. It is generally believed that if more then five lymph nodes are infected the patient's chances for long-term control are minimal. Some experts will say that there is no chance of surviving beyond a five year period if as many as 15 lymph nodes are involved.

Peggy did not want conventional therapy (chemotherapy) so Warner mapped out a program using predominantly BCG and other immune enhancing agents. These were biologic materials that were stimulating her immune system. Over a period of a year, she was free of any evidence of recurrent disease. She was a patient before the time tumor markers were used so Warner had to depend upon such things as a general physical examination and x-rays, which today are fairly crude methods of follow-up. This patient has never had any further difficulty. She changed her attitude and her exercise program and even though she went through some very trying situations she was immunologically strong enough to keep her tumor under control. Peggy has been in remission for over twenty years and Warner believed that the use of BCG was a factor in her survival.

He believed that the fact that the tumor and all of her lymph nodes were removed could not be accepted as the reason for her success because it is known that cancer is a systemic disease. It is not a surgical disease. Initially, it is one that starts spreading long before it ever becomes symptomatic. For this reason, there had to be some other factor going on and the only other thing that was done was strengthening her immune system. He did make things better from a psychological standpoint. He relieved a lot of the things that might have been immunosuppressive, but also, actively, through BCG and bacterial vaccines, stimulated her immune system to work harder and become stronger.

*　　　*　　　*　　　*

BCG was used throughout Warner's practice when he believed it might be helpful to the patient. It was a substance which had been used for many years in millions of people. The side effects, if any, were known and it had been demonstrated to be of value in tumors. It was under constant study by major universities and for this reason he used it in an investigative manner to find out in how many areas and how many different ways it would be beneficial. Because it is a benign substance, it was worth trying.

BCG is better known then other bacterial vaccines because there is such a long record of its use. The side effects, if any, are known and there is better knowledge on how to use it in treatment. Any systemic infection can be treated effectively with BCG. There are other vaccines that could possibly have the same results, but the response to their use has been unacceptable to the patient. They produced ulcerations and infections that were far greater than any caused by BCG. The side effects of BCG in his treatment program were minimal.

When tumor markers became available, they were an important tool in tracking tumor activity and evaluating the success of treatment. As mentioned previously, tumor markers are glyco proteins that develop on the surface of tumor cells and are peculiar to that tumor cell and not to the normal cell. For this reason, its presence indicates that the particular tumor is someplace in the body or the process that results in that stimulation is producing that kind of reaction. These indicators can be picked up by special means in the laboratory in a relatively easy manner. The results are used as a monitor of response to therapy, the presence of disease and relapse. It is an excellent way of screening. There are other things that turn up in the blood that can be evaluated and are seen mostly in breast cancers.

Tumor markers are not considered specific enough because there have not been sufficient studies. Therefore, Warner was not given official approval for their use as a routine agent. He believed that tumor markers could be used by a practitioner who understood their value in diagnosis and monitoring treatment. There is no harm to the patient who agrees to this test and they were never used without informed consent. The main objection has always been that because the doctor is waiting to evaluate the results of the tumor markers he may deny the chance that the patient would respond to the immediate use of surgery, radiation or chemotherapy.

There is a great deal of difference in the breast cancer of pre-menopausal or postmenopausal patients. The patient is more hormonally active in the premenopausal state and the hormone levels are beginning to drop off in the postmenopausal state. If it is a hormone-induced tumor, then in a postmenopausal state the incentives or the cause to factors to make the tumor would be less severe then they were in the premenopausal patient. There seems to be more aggressive tumor in the premenopausal and more difficulty controlling it although there will be more breast cancer in postmenopausal women.

The treatment program varied depending on the severity of the disease. With early premenopausal tumors, there is a great deal of therapy that can be done for patients to control the tumor. If the tumor has progressed to a point where it is widely or massively invading other structures, quite often there is very little that can be done to stop its growth. Then it is necessary to get the person to learn to live constructively with what tumor they have. However, the postmenopausal woman that responds well and often dramatically to hormone manipulation does not need the aggressive therapies.

Postmenopausal women have a low estrogen level and if this is an estrogen induced tumor, the lower estrogen levels would lead to less continuous stimulation of the tumor. One of the things to remember is that the postmenopausal women has become symptomatic of a process that started a long time ago. It may have even started at the minute she started menstruating when the breasts undergo changes of the alternating hormone levels that occur. It takes that long to develop just as all men will likely get a prostatic carcinoma if they live long enough.

*   *   *   *

Over time, it was possible to evaluate patients' responses to various modalities. It was found that of the three major treatment programs the only one that really gave the information needed was the surgical approach. It is not always the surgery that removes the tumor; it is the information provided by the surgery. This information allowed Warner to pursue treatments with immunotherapy, genetic therapy, and other biologic means where there was a specific effect on the tumor cell. Or, at least, enough of an effect on the tumor cells without damaging the normal system that gave the patient a chance of survival. That has been the case up to now. For this reason, the patient needs to be aware that there are alternative treatments which are different then the approaches previously used.

In other words, healing does not always come from what the doctor does, but it comes from what we make the body or help the body do to heal itself. It is the immune system, the body's own defense mechanism, its own protective systems that overcome the disease process. The physician may help buy time. Quite often the side effects of radiation and chemotherapy are greater than the benefits. The use of these investigative, aggressive programs can produce changes that make it irreconcilable for many other treatment programs such as stimulating the immune system and making the body stronger.

Warner saw his role as a physician as a coach, suggesting and encouraging. A physician is a teacher. He tries to explain the disease to the patient in a way that they will learn that there are people who have succeeded. As an advocate for the patients, the physician teaches them that they have a big part in the healing process. If they make the right choices and work at lifestyle changes, it is possible to stop the carcinogenic process and leads to tumor control. Also, perhaps it will slow down the growth of the tumor and the good quality of life and prolonged disease free interval will be extended by this approach.

$$*\qquad*\qquad*\qquad*$$

Particularly difficult cases of breast cancer are the ones that have already metastasized (spread to another part of the body). A different approach is needed in this instance. It is important to use as many different approaches as possible and to know how the patient is responding. The blood count is needed in order to know if the immune system is remaining strong. Blood chemistries tell the doctor if the body organs are functioning normally and if the patient is producing abnormal chemicals as a result of the presence of tumor. Rising tumor markers indicate the patient is in trouble or that the treatment program is not working. These cases are challenging, but not impossible to get under control.

*   *   *   *

One case history of this nature was that of Louise (name changed). I first saw her in 1973 when her breast cancer had metastasized to the bone in the pelvic area. She had received a radical mastectomy in 1969 with no cancer found in the lymph system. At that time, she was pronounced cured and no follow-up treatment was recommended. With her consent, I treated her with BCG, a male hormone and lifestyle changes. She had minimal side effects, the quality of her life was excellent and she remains cancer free.

*   *   *   *

Warner tailored the treatment to the individual patient. He used what he considered to be the best of conventional and complementary medicine. Every case was different, but he never considered that any was impossible. Warner commented that he thinks most doctors will admit that it is a mystery why some patients survive and others with the same problem do not.

CHAPTER 10

PROSTATE CANCER

Prostatic carcinoma is not unlike breast carcinoma in females. They are both hormonally dependent tumors and they have a good response to hormones. When hormones are properly used, they give a prolonged disease free interval and quality of life that is not obtainable by more aggressive therapies.

This more conservative course in the treatment of prostatic carcinoma is based on studies which show that 87% of the men using this protocol have not had any further problem for an average of ten years. At that time, any signs of relapse can be dealt with in much the same manner as they would have been dealt with originally, but the patient has had a long interval of no treatment and a higher quality of life. Two studies of large numbers of men have confirmed this. It was also Warner's experience that a quality of life and longevity can be obtained that is far greater then that obtained by a surgical or radiation approach.

Surgery is not a good approach as a prostate cancer treatment. Surgeons often tell patients they "got it all", but it is very difficult to encompass the entire lesion, either because the extent of the neoplasm is difficult to see, or because the tumor cells have already spread. Telling someone the tumor can be removed surgically flies in the face of our current knowledge regarding the biology of cancer. Tumor cells start flaking off the tumor mass long before the tumor mass becomes symptomatic.

There are many factors that need to be considered in the initial meeting with the patient with prostate cancer. Certainly, the age at which a man gets this tumor will influence to a great extent the value of the treatment selected. Since nearly all men eventually get a prostatic carcinoma if they live long enough, it becomes more of an aging process than an induced aberration in cellular growth in that individual. So, if the individual is beyond 65 and with a longevity of an additional fifteen years, it will be possible to do the therapy without an aggressive approach. Using this watchful waiting period, checking the PSA at approximately monthly intervals for the first three months and every three months thereafter, one can be reasonably sure that the course of the illness is being adequately followed. (PSA stands for Prostatic Specific Antigen, which is a protein on the surface of the tumor cell that is different than the normal cell membrane proteins. These proteins are what is called a tumor marker and serves as an indicator of the amount of tumor present. When measured by blood tests at regular intervals, it is possible to monitor the success of treatment).

As mentioned earlier, at least two large studies show that 87% of the men who have had a diagnosis of prostatic carcinoma and who had no subsequent aggressive therapy, went ten years before evidence of exacerbation of their disease occurred. Warner believed these statistics could be even further improved if one would use supportive measures such as the exercise, diet and complementary measures that have been demonstrated to show some deterrent effect on prostatic stimulation. Since elevation of the testosterone seems to be a significant factor in the production of prostatic growth, relieving stress becomes an increasingly important way to reduce the gonadtrophic hormones that elevates testosterone secretion.

Of special interest regarding the timing of therapy initiation, is a study done at Wayne State University of healthy men under 50 who had been killed in accidents. Prostate cancer was found in 45 per cent of these unfortunate people. Clearly, this indicates that each treatment plan must be individualized. Patients deserve a more thoughtful, well planned treatment approach rather than the cookbook approach too often applied to all who are diagnosed with prostate carcinoma.

*   *   *   *

Surgery should be used only when there is a very small well controlled focal lesion centrally located away from the capsule. Impotence, incontinence, and urinary frequency too often result from surgery. Because there is only a five year general level of control for most surgical patients, this approach, in Warner's opinion, was not justified in view of the longevity and quality of life that can be obtained by other measures.

Many times it is felt that a radiation approach should be offered. It does appear it has fewer side effects, but again the five year control rate approximates that of surgery. The amount of radiation necessary to control the tumor can cause damage to the rectum and bladder. Such severe side effects destroy the effectiveness of this approach. Although it is true that dose levels can be controlled by giving external radiation combined with seed implants, there is a significant five year failure rate that begins a year or so after the five year interval. Because of the specialized training of radiation oncologists, this procedure often has to be done at a city distant from the patient's residence.

Because elevated testosterone levels lead to the repetitive stimulation and growth of the abnormal prostate cells until they finally acquire the capacity to grow on their own and become invasive, it was necessary to find some way to reduce testosterone levels. Stress reduction was one way this could be done. This can be accomplished by reducing the amount of dihydroepiandrosterone (DHE) that is formed under stressful situations. Reduction of dietary animal fat also reduces the presence of many precursors that can be converted into testosterone. However, of greater importance is the reduction of the gonadtrophic hormone by the pituitary's action on the testicles to make testosterone by using leuprolide (Lupron, Zolodex). At first there will be some increased blood flow in the area of the tumor, local tenderness and irritability. An increase in symptoms of urinary distress might occur through the adrenal glands being stimulated at the same time producing more testosterone. This activity can be blocked by use of two medications taken by mouth, namely Casodex taken once a day or Flutamide tablets every 8 hours.

Many practitioners have found that these distressing side effects will disappear with the use of the oral medication over a period of two to three weeks. Then they can be discontinued leaving only the monthly shots. Warner preferred the monthly shots the first three months in order that the PSA could be checked and to make sure the patient is responding to therapy. But of greater importance was the reassurance to the patient that he was being watched, that his doctor was interested in the course of his illness, and available to answer the many questions that will be coming up as he talks to other people who have similar problems or have gone through the treatment programs and may have had different results. These are questions that the patient needs answered for his personal confidence that he selected the right treatment. If all is going well and the PSA is dropping, the doctor can use the longer acting form of the antagonist (Lupron or Zolodex) and give a shot every three months.

There are now many support groups made up of men with prostatic carcinoma. These groups have a lot of information which when shared reassures individuals with the disease and helps them to develop an understanding of the carcinoma process and the value of the treatment they have chosen.

After a period of time, in which the PSA has been under one (1), meaning testosterone levels are very low, and there is no evidence of extension beyond the gland and other enzymes noted on the blood chemistries are within normal range, the patient can be assured that the disease is in remission. The recommendation would then be that individuals then begin to explore the possibility of using small amounts of the hormone suppressors (Lupron and Zolodex) of testosterone production and extending the time between the shots.

*   *   *   *

The patient must be aware that there is a down side to the use of these powerful medicines. Psychologically, for many men, the most serious is the loss of sexual function. With the reduction or elimination of testosterone, the patient is essentially castrated. Unlike surgical castration, however, this condition is reversible with reduction or elimination of the use of Lupron. Lupron can also cause bone loss (osteoporosis), a condition which may require other therapy to control.

It is here that the art of medicine plays the crucial role. Doctors must know how to balance the fact that Lupron is the best therapy available for many cases of prostate cancer against these undesirable side effects. In Warner's judgment, the value outweighed the negatives overwhelmingly.

Careful follow-up at semi-annual intervals is necessary to insure that control of the cancer is maintained. As Lupron is withdrawn, normal male characteristics such as bone growth and increased bone density accompanied by increased muscular activity will reduce the incidence of osteoporosis. Normal martial relationships will again be possible. Some patients have reported improvement in mental status and emotional stability as the drug is withdrawn. Continuing on with a good exercise program, getting adequate rest, following the other complementary measures to maintain good health and immune stimulation may maintain this period of disease control over a period of many years. Only by careful, semi-annual evaluations can the patient be sure that this remission will be continued.

Another valuable therapy is cryo surgery, in which liquid nitrogen is used to freeze the tumor, the prostate and the tissue around the prostate. This will control tumor growth. The value of cyro surgery is limited, however, because only a few specialists in a few U. S. cities know this technique, and consequently it is not generally available.

Continuing to gain meaningful information through support groups, the internet, and individual reading, the patient can improve his feeling of well being. Through these activities he becomes aware that only a small part of his body is not functioning properly. The vast majority of his body functions are normal and they have the capacity to develop an environment that is very harmful to the tumor but very beneficial for the individual, helping him to heal and live a happy, purposeful life. Absence of carcinoma of the prostate does not seem to be a significant factor. It is preventing the process from continuing on growing.

*   *   *   *

The more the patient can combine knowledge, stress reduction and spiritual activity to make his internal body work more efficiently, the more he is using the normal healing potential of his own body to deal with the tumor problem. The body does not want to be sick and it is only our activities that prevent the body from the healing that it can do. A study of large groups of men using this philosophical approach has demonstrated that a better quality of life, extended periods of disease control, and prolonged years of survival makes this the treatment of choice for an individual with carcinoma of the prostate.

CHAPTER 11

MELANOMA TREATMENT

Melanoma is a rapidly growing tumor that quite often causes a very short life span for the patient. If the right treatment is not used originally, the result will probably be disastrous. For this reason, it became a main focus of Warner's investigation and research regarding the many ways to treat this form of cancer and, in general, other tumors.

When Warner first started practicing medicine very little was known about the diagnosis and treatment of melanoma other then a surgical approach and that was often a very radical surgical approach. If the patient had a small lesion on the thigh or the foot, the surgeon would amputate. Cancer is not a surgical disease so the results were never very good. As time went on, the incidence of melanoma was rising which was attributed to more exposure of the body to sunlight or the development of severe sunburns earlier in adolescence or early adult life. This led to frequent development of a black mole that grew fairly rapidly and if not removed at the right time could get the patient in serious difficulty.

In making a diagnosis, a dermatologist could usually look at the lesion and tell whether or not it was melanoma or some other skin disease and treat it appropriately. However, it was always better to get a pathologic diagnosis. A histologic diagnosis by a pathologist tells the treating physician the kind of lesion present; whether it is a benign tumor or something else. If it was confirmed to be a melanoma, it would need to be biopsied. The biopsy removed a significant amount of normal tissue around the lesion. This procedure did not have to be as radical as it used to be. The surgeon used to take two or three inches around the lesion and then use a skin graft. This approach has been shown to be unnecessary as it did not improve overall statistics.

What often alerted the patient to see a doctor was a change in the appearance of a lesion. If the individual was informed about the early signs of malignant change in melanoma, he would immediately see a doctor to have the lesion checked out. Most of the time these are asympotmatic. The ones that get large and are bleeding usually present a more serious diagnosis. These symptoms usually mean that the tumor has invaded into the deeper structures and, therefore, the prognosis is poor. Other then itching, color changes and sometimes the appearance of a halo, a whitened patch around the lesion indicative of the immune system working, there are no other early signs.

Warner's interest was sparked by the fact that there was knowledge about the life span of the tumor. That is, how long it would take until it started doing predictable things. Secondly, it was right out on the surface where it could be observed. So it was an ideal tumor to study using immunologic tools. It was for this reason, that he became so interested in melanoma tumors while he was at the Tumor Institute. The time was around 1969-1970.

Utilizing immunologic types of procedure, he could follow predictable levels of tumor markers to see if the treatment he was using were satisfactorily influencing the disease. About this time, there was a great deal of information coming from Dr. Raap of the National Cancer Institute who noted that there was a response when the melanoma was injected with the BCG vaccine. This was the same bovine tuberculosis organism that was used in other immunologic modulations in treating other cancers. With the use of BCG, Warner was able to produce favorable changes in melanoma patients. It became apparent that it was an immunologically alterable disease and that surgery was of value only if it was done early. Radiation therapy was of little or no value because the cells seemed to be resistant and they required different kinds of doses of radiation to make any change, which was more or less intolerable to normal tissues.

The cytotoxic chemotherapy approach tried through the Southwest Oncology Group for a number of years used every combination of every drug. The Group had data from thousands of melanoma patients collected from all over the United States. Various other types of therapy were tried and they failed to show any significant improvement. Dr. Constanzi was the principal investigator. Eventually, after he had analyzed the work completed over a 10 to 15 year period, he came to the conclusion that cytotoxic chemotherapy drugs probably produced a 17% alteration in the course of the illness, but did not significantly prolong survival time. For this reason, only the surgical approach showed any long-term benefits. Since this was a disease on the surface and one that could be diagnosed early and appropriate therapy started, it was an ideal tumor to use in the initial studies of the BCG program.

*   *   *   *

Melanoma does have a peculiar history when it first appears. In other words, some melanomas will spontaneously disappear although that is probably less then 10% of them if it's that high. Things can happen to the body that will cause a resolution of the tumor without any medical intervention and that, too, is an unknown that is an infrequent finding. At other times, the surgeon could surgically remove the cancer and if adequate margins around he tumor were removed, there did not seem to be any further problem. Given this kind of a growth history, it became apparent that careful diagnosing and evaluating the treatments that were given that showed improvement were due to the therapy administered. In order to do this, it was necessary to go back to the time that the histologic pattern was developed. This could be used in diagnosis and would give a fairly good idea about whether or not the tumor was going to be something that could be manipulated.

This pattern had four stages and when the melanoma cells were compliant and confined to the upper portion of the skin, it was called level A. Level B was when the malignancy was down to the general layer of the skin, C when it was into the meticular dermis, and D into the papillary dermis. All of these are levels on the skin itself. They are very thin and needed a microscope in order to determine the depth of invasion. Knowing the depth of invasion, the thickness of the lesion could be measured from the bottom to the top. This was fairly reliable as another prognostic indicator.

The surgeon would provide a specimen and from this information it could be determined whether the treatment had to be fairly aggressive early or if there was a possibility of using other kinds of therapy. Perhaps the specimen would also tell what the prognosis would be. So diagnosis became very important from the pathology standpoint. The main reason this was important was if the tumor was confined then the chances of control were very good. The earlier and the less invasion the more likely that the tumor could be controlled. If the tumor went down beneath the skin into the fatty layers or spread to the local lymph nodes, it was a Stage 2 tumor and the prognosis dropped precipitously. If it had spread to other parts of the body, survival was usually measured in times of six months to a year. This evaluation was always completed prior to any kind of therapy the patient received. The surgeons tried extensive lymph nodes dissection and wide excisions of the areas and they found in very large studies that it did not have any beneficial effects and probably contributed to the dissemination of the disease.

There was one successful program done in Dallas for awhile in which the attending physician perfused the area by injecting cytotoxic chemotherapy agents that were available at the time into the blood stream. It was a very technical procedure, but there was some control of the disease using this procedure. However, it was not readily available because of the extreme need that had to be presented. After getting more information about the effects of immunologic approaches, Warner felt that this was the most favorable approach.

Lymphocyte sensitivity to the tumor cell was demonstrated, the presence of cytotoxic antibodies in the patient's blood that could kill the tumor. Many of the very early findings of immunotherapy treatment for cancer developed from the many research projects that were done throughout the nation and at most of the major medical centers. The diagnostic procedures mentioned were used and also various immune programs most of which included BCG, the vaccine.

* * * *

Warner became very involved with these studies because he could supply clinical material to the Hellstrom team. Drs. Karl and Ingegerd Hellstrom were the ones who developed most of the basic information that is known about the lymphocytes and the reactions of the drug to the tumor and other blood studies. These studies gave additional information on how the patient was responding to therapy.

Somewhat serendipitively, Dr. Karl Hellstrom noted that there were certain patients in the program where the expected result did not occur. It did not appear to make any sense according to all the things that were known. Dr. Hellstrom laboriously checked the reasons for this and found out that the ones who had an unusual response that he could not explain were blacks. African Americans do not get melanoma except in the white areas of their body so he thought it was possible that they carried a blocking factor that was responsible for their not getting this type of cancer. This led to the use of plasma taken from the blood of healthy black people without any evidence of tumors. This blood was then injected into patients with advanced melanoma to see if it would have any affect on the tumor.

The Hellstroms were able to isolate eight different antigens that are present in almost all melanomas. There might be a different pattern in various ones, but it could serve as a diagnostic procedure. There was a good possibility that making a monoclonal antibody against a particular antigen could develop a good treatment program. This occurred in 1979. The Hellstroms and Warner were working with the University of

Washington at the time. Then the National Cancer Institute (NCI) in Washington, D.C. hired the entire University group. Everyone connected to the program went to the NCI and this included doctors, residents, nurses and many of the technicians involved in the program. As a result, there was no follow-up in Seattle and the NCI group has never used the material that was developed at the Tumor Institute. (For a more detailed discussion of the melanoma study, see Chapter 3).

Warner did not know what the politics were at that time—why the material was never used. Other research circles have utilized the same material. The UCLA Medical School is pushing the program used by Warner. They have proven the value of this kind of vaccine as well as other biologic response modifiers including BCG. They found out independently and from Warner's work with the Hellstroms and it is in general use at UCLA. It is now the treatment of choice, but for the past of five or more years the treatment can only be obtained at UCLA. They will let local doctors follow through on patients, but the administration of the vaccine is done exclusively at UCLA. Because of this policy, Warner sent patients to UCLA to receive the vaccine.

With the information received from the research study conducted at Fred Hutchinson Cancer Research Center, (FHCRC), he continued with the use of BCG and he was using it in other treatment programs. He felt that he should continue his program because he felt there was a significant improvement that he could not explain. However, he could see that his patients were living, tumors were regressing, their quality of life was much better and overall they were doing better treated with this program than with anything else offered at the time.

*   *   *   *

Warner attempted to get statistical reports that demonstrated the efficacy of this approach. In 1984 he asked the Fred Hutchinson research statistical department to look at his material and make records of it and to help him follow this data. It was on this basis he began to see that the benefits still continued and there were other things he could add that would make a difference in the therapy. That spurred him on to continue the investigative treatment of melanoma often using things that were not regulated, but were shown to be of value in the treatment of malignant disease. He compiled a treatment regimen that was very successful in a large number of people.

With the information acquired, it became apparent that some of patients were getting well with a wide variety of therapies. Warner was open to any program he learned about. There were people all over the world trying various approaches in melanoma because it was readily prevalent and had such a poor prognosis. There were studies that showed that anytime the immune system was stimulated, there was a significant improvement in the course of the melanoma.

Different approaches were tried. Non-specific vaccines from ordinary bacteria or viruses that challenged the immune system were administered. Immune response to the vaccine could be measured and showed that there was improvement. Also, the lymphocytes could be measured and it was noted that there was a rise in the T cell population and, specifically, the helper cells, which are responsible for starting the immune reaction against the tumor. Warner believed all of this pointed to the fact that there was an immunologic approach and if the right combination could be found, it would be successful.

Given the fact that Warner had this immune program, and the fact that he demonstrated in a large number of his patients who are living as long as twenty years after the therapies that were available at the time, he knew that it was a treatable disease. It needed to be treated, the doctor needed to understand the disease and the cooperation and commitment of the patient was essential. Unless melanoma is properly treated in the early stages, it progresses fairly rapidly.

Most of the time when a person has widespread melanoma they are considered terminal within a short time. Warner had patients with melanoma who had had several surgical procedures and later had recurrences of metastatic disease. He treated them with the vaccine.

*   *   *   *

There was a dairy farmer in this area who had many, many melanoma lesions surgically removed from his body. He was given the vaccine and since that time, he has not developed any tumors on the skin. He developed lymph node metastases and a couple of times lymph nodes were removed that proved the presence of malignancy. He had lung metastases and with the vaccine these all disappeared. He is now well beyond a period of fifteen years since his original diagnosis was established. He works full time as a dairy farmer, but remains on the vaccine.

*   *   *   *

Another lady treated had a large melanoma on her heel that was removed by surgery on a couple of occasions. She developed metastases in the lymph nodes in the groin as a result of the spread of the tumor and these were removed. Following this, she had swelling in her leg. In addition to this, there were black tumor nodules scattered throughout the skin of the lower extremity. Many of these were injected with BCG and later on with interferon. There was a complete resolution of the problem. There is no evidence of any of those black skin nodules, which were injected with BCG and interferon. This woman is in her 60's and lives in the Seattle area. She was treated for over a year, but she quit coming when she lost her means of income and could not pay for the therapy. There was no evidence of tumor, but she was asked to come in periodically for evaluation.

*   *   *   *

Another patient was a young, healthy contractor in very good health. He was a vigorous individual in his mid 30s who had developed multiple lesions over his back. Those were surgically removed and then Warner sent him to UCLA in Los Angeles. He had lymph node involvement under both arms, which responded to the treatment with the vaccine. His nodes were biopsied and showed the presence of melanoma. He subsequently developed liver metastases when he was on extended maintenance follow-ups every 3 to 6 months. He then went back to UCLA where they resected the liver lesions and he is free of disease, continues on the vaccine and works full time as a heavy construction contractor.

*   *   *   *

Another patient had a melanoma on the heel of his foot. His melanoma did not have the black characteristics. Unfortunately, it was biopsied repeatedly and the repeated manipulation of the tumor by surgical means usually leads to a loss of control and spreading of the tumor. This happened to this patient. He continued to do fairly well for a long period of time then the tumor spread to his skin, the lymph nodes and to his lower abdomen. He remained on the vaccine up until a month or so before his death. Death was apparently due to the tremendous amount of tumor that developed in the lower abdomen. His quality of life was good. He felt that the vaccine was helping him so he continued. BCG vaccine was used in the last year of his life, injecting it directly into nodules and this seemed to produce a severe inflammatory reaction, but also boosted his immune reaction against the tumor.

*   *   *   *

Still another patient was a restaurateur from Portland who was in his mid 30s. He had a number of skin nodules that began on the chest wall. They metastasized to lymph nodes on both sides of the axillary under the arm some of which could be removed, some not. Radiation was tried and was unsuccessful. Then he was sent to the clinic at UCLA because BCG could be given here, but the UCLA vaccine was only available there. This patient has been going to UCLA for well over five years and he has not had any other serious problems. His tumors are apparently in remission. He talks to other patients all the time about the wonderful things that are happening.

*   *   *   *

Thirty years ago there was a patient who had a melanoma of the foot and the surgical approach at that time was to do partial amputation. Her therapy consisted of BCG and some changes in her diet program. Warner said that she would be one of those persons where it was not known whether the immune approach contributed to her good result. Warner did know that with many patients if they were given just a little bit of immunotherapy, it would be enough to trigger the immune system to work harder and overcome the disease.

*   *   *   *

There was a nurse who had skin involvement and had two episodes of tumor involvement in the small bowel one of which resulted in severe bleeding at the point of obstruction. She had to have a resection and then received BCG therapy. She worked on her lifestyle and a number of other things. She continued working for a long time as a nurse at the University of Washington. She subsequently had two children and is currently free of disease.

No one knows for sure the causes of melanoma, but it seems to be reactions to the ultra violet rays and specific portions of the ultra violet ray spectrum that produces DNA damage. This produces a mutant cell which, if not removed or destroyed, continues to grow until it destroys the individual.

In addition to BCG, the use of interferon as an immune stimulant has been available for a good many years. It is a cytokine, a hormone-like substance secreted by the lymphocytes, which are responsible for initiating immune reactions against tumors. They are also responsible for other cytokines such as interleukins developed by the lymph nodes. A cascading effect develops so that you can go from many different types of interleukins and cytokines, also known as lymphokines that will demonstrate the effectiveness on the part of the body to control the tumor. Interferon is produced naturally in the body, but it can also be synthesized and injected. It is possible that BCG stimulates the lymphocytes to make interferon.

Melanoma is a tumor that lends itself very well to immunologic investigation. Because most of the lesions can be seen, it is easier to study. In summary, melanoma is an extraordinarily deadly form of cancer that responds very well to immunological treatment. At least 70% of the patients will live a significant number of years with this type of therapy. They will have a good quality of life without aggressive treatment.

There are many places in the United States that have seen the advantages and benefits that have been obtained at UCLA and are developing their own vaccines. In Warner's opinion, there are many medical people who are not aware of what can be done for the melanoma patient. They have not read the extensive literature on this subject and so do not give their patients appropriate treatment.

Any major city will have an oncologist and it depends upon his training as to what he recommends. If he follows the conventional approach, which I think in many places is chemotherapy, (cytotoxic drugs), then the patient will not get the proper treatment. If the doctor has had immunologic exposure, which most of them do not have or have rejected, the patient is not going to get the treatment that is available. Just because it is a major medical center does not insure that you are going to get the immunology approach because many of the major medical centers still do not believe in immune therapy as a means of treating any tumor.

CHAPTER 12

LUNG CANCER

Most of the time the initial symptoms of lung cancer are chronic cough, shortness of breath with exertion, or a general malaise and fatigue. The byproducts of the tumor are beginning to interfere with normal metabolic function of the body and the patient begins to lose weight, appetite is not good and he is not sleeping well. It varies from very specific to non-specific symptoms. It is up to the physician to be aware of the possibilities.

Any or all of these symptoms would lead to the suspicion that this patient could have lung cancer. It is necessary to rule out other associated illnesses like a heart problem, asthmatic condition, or a chronic infection with appropriate tests. Other factors in the patient's past history such as smoking and alcoholism should be determined. Alcoholism contributes to lung cancer because of its immunosuppressive activities.

Necessary tests include a chest x-ray, blood counts to see if there is a blood loss problem associated with the disease or whether or not there is a sign of infection. The blood chemistries help determine what the other organisms of the body are doing in response to the presence of a growth in the lungs and show abnormalities in the enzymes that will indicate whether there is tissue destruction in the body. The tests may not tell where the problem is located, but it will alert the doctor to the fact that the patient has a chronic problem. It should be noted whether or not protein levels are adequate. This will give some idea whether or not malnutrition is a factor. The patient would have been ill for a long period of time for this became a factor.

After the initial tests, tumor markers can be used. The CEA, (carcinogenic, embryonic antigen), may be valuable. It is a fetal like protein that is turned off when the individual is born. When malignancies develop, the oncogene that makes this will be stimulated to grow and may be rising.

Sometimes lung cancer is the result of metastases (spread) from a primary tumor located in another part of the body. The only way this can be determined is to get a piece of the tumor. In this day and age, it is possible, through fine needle aspiration, to obtain a tiny segment of the tumor from the lung to determine whether it is malignant. If it is malignant, some of the characteristics may give a hint as to where it is originating. If it originated in the lung, it would have a different characteristic then if it had metastasized to the lung. It depends upon the cellular component from which the original tumor grew. There are certain types of tissue that should not be in the lung that would be picked up with the biopsy and that would indicate that it is from some distant area.

There is some risk in the case of lung cancer or any other cancer of focusing the treatment on that malignancy and having it rage out of control in some other part of the body. This depends on the kind of treatment. If suppressive treatments were used, it was possible that the tumor would grow more readily in other areas and the primary site that was different then the lung. More particularly, the primary site would continue to grow and cause trouble unless it was recognized. One of the first things done in the initial work up and treatment of the cancer patient was to reduce the volume of tumor as much as possible.

The diagnosis identifies the kind of tumor, the pattern of growth, what the body is doing against the tumor and what the tumor is doing to the body. Surgery is the major treatment that can do any significant good for the patient with lung cancer. The reason is that surgery gives the doctor information as to the kind of tumor and the growth patterns of the tumor. It tells the doctor what the tumor is doing to the body. In other words, is the body being immunosuppressed by the tumor, what is the body's reaction against it, is the patient manufacturing antibodies against the tumor antigen and how aggressive the tumor is in attacking the bodies metabolic functions. These are the kind of things that will be used to determine the kind of treatment program recommended for the patient. If a resection of a portion of the lung is not possible because of the extensive area of the tumor, the possibilities of doing any long-term control are not good.

If the tumor is in the periphery or central area of the lung where the surgeon can remove it and a portion of the bronchus, then there is a chance that surgery would be of value. If it is deep in the lung involving other lobes or spread across some of the tissue planes, then the possibility of getting it out is not good even if you remove the whole lung. During surgery, it is possible that not enough tumor cells are present in any one spot to give a finding on the x-ray or the CT scan. This makes it possible to think everything is out, but in reality some clinical disease may remain after the surgery. Because of this, the chances of excising everything are small.

Beyond surgery, there are not too many choices although some patients have responded to other approaches that do not harm the body. This would be such things as biologic response modifiers, interferons, interluekins, and tissue necrosing factor. These stimulate the immune system and sometimes, by judicious use of extra amounts of the cytokines, a substance the body manufactures to kill tumor, the course of the illness can be altered.

Lung cancer is the one that is the least responsive to treatment. Even though we know causative factors, these causative factors have been present for so long that the chances of preventive medicine helping are very limited. This is especially true in the tobacco related lung tumors. Still, there are a significant number of people who have developed lung tumors who are non-smokers. There are other factors beyond this chronic irritation that produces this response resulting in a tumor.

*   *   *   *

After the diagnosis is made, the first thing in selecting a treatment program is to make the body stronger. Then concentration must be on how to make the immune system stronger and, finally, to find ways to reduce the volume of tumor. The immune system can help fight it and, perhaps, medication given will give the body time enough to develop antibodies against the tumor and destroy it.

BCG is valuable as an agent for strengthening the immune system. Warner felt it would be beneficial for lung cancer if the injections were given when the chest was open and the doctor could see the regional lymph nodes draining the tumor area. These nodes received the BCG injection and there was an inflammatory response. For a period of six to nine months, there was measurable improvement in the people who had the BCG injections. Then the tumors often began to recur. Obviously, the tumor situation was helped by the immune stimulation. This procedure was not continued mainly because the surgeon did not feel he could inject through the chest wall and into these areas with enough accuracy to get a high enough dose into that area again. If he had injected each of those areas every six months, then there may have been enough stimuli to keep the tumor under control and for the body to mount an antibody response against the tumor sufficient to overcome the disease.

This protocol was dropped shortly after it was started because it was obvious that there was only a short-term advantage that could not be continued unless the BCG was reintroduced deep in the lymphatic near the tumor site. That was not possible without doing an open thoracotomy, (surgical incision of the chest wall), which was unacceptable.

New techniques of diagnosis enable the surgeon to do an endoscopic examination with a telescopic lens through the rib cage inside the chest and look directly at the outside of the tumor. Then the tumor can be biopsied. There are ways a skilled surgeon can remove that tumor just through that tiny opening and perhaps control the disease. It was not feasible to think in terms of reinjecting through that tube because of the number of times it would be necessary to give an adequate dose of BCG. Warner believed it would be possible with x-ray and other localization studies to find out where the tumor was and put needles in from the outside that intersect through the area of the tumor. Then BCG could be injected into that tumor that would help the immune system recognize that there is an abnormal group of cells growing. This would help from the standpoint of overcoming the tolerance that seems to develop. In other words, the body learns that there is an abnormality that it has to put up with. Then the body doesn't mount an immune response to kill that tumor so the tumor continues to grow. There are ways that tolerances develop in the body that prevents the immune system from destroying the tumor.

So the diagnosis was made and then an effort was made to make the body as strong as possible, first by stimulating the immune system. That could take up to three weeks. At the end of that time, the surgeon removed as much tumor as possible. During the surgery, the surgeon could also determine if the patient was having a positive response to medications being used. From that standpoint, the surgery and the endoscopic evaluations are very important.

*   *   *   *

Most of the therapy would be directed at staying away from those causative factors that might be responsible for the production of the cancer. Again, the carcinogenic process is the important thing. It was not the symptoms and the development of a mass in a particular location that was the most important thing. It was what caused that cell to develop in the first place that had to be stopped or regardless of what was done it would to continue to act and the tumor will recur. The question always was why didn't the body recognize that there was an abnormality that should not be there and mount an antibody, hormone or an anti-tumor response on the part of the body that would destroy the tumor?

It is known that there are some people who do surprisingly well with or without treatment. There was the classic case in Seattle that was featured in the Seattle P. I. newspaper for a number of years about an individual who was seen at the Veterans Administration Hospital. The diagnosis of lung cancer was well established at the University of Washington. The patient had an open chest operation that showed the surgeons could not get around the lesion. A small amount of the tumor was removed but not really all of it. Surgery was followed by radiation treatment and his tumor apparently grew while he was on radiation. The patient had some chemotherapy, which made him very ill and was discontinued by the patient. He became a farmer on Bainbridge Island. Every year there would be a follow-up on him and he did reasonably well taking care of himself on the farm for over ten years. There was no follow-up after the ten year period, but he went that length of time knowing he had a serious disease for which nothing could be done. That case is contrasted with 99% of cases where the patient may have had surgery or been told there was no effective treatment. Most of these patients died within less then a year.

There are other people who have been treated by giving radiation treatment in large chunks once a week. We had one patient who went well beyond twelve years with his tumor before he developed another kind of tumor that could have been the result of the radiation treatment. After responding for about five years to unconventional therapy, he made a decision to undergo conventional therapy using chemotherapy agents in the year he died.

The general consensus of opinion nowadays is that radiation therapy is not effective except to stop pain, bleeding and maybe reduce obstruction. The surgeons who do good work with lung tumors are capable of putting laser beams down through the bronchoscope or tubes that go directly into the lungs and the tumor. By putting these anti-tumor agents right into tumors, they are more likely to have a significant influence on the tumor. However, this procedure gives only temporary relief and must be repeated at three to six month intervals depending on the speed that the tumor grows. Warner did not see any permanent remission from this procedure.

*   *   *   *

Warner did not have many long-term survivors who were diagnosed with lung cancer, but there were some. He recalled one patient who lived over twelve years without any significant problem with his cancer. He gave this patient high dose radiation for four weeks and then no other treatment except BCG as a maintenance therapy. In this case, radiation was the crucial treatment because surgery was not an option.

There have been other people who have been survivors. Many of these were individuals who refused to give in to their disease. As they kept fighting, it was amazing how long they prolonged the inevitable outcome. In other words, there were disease free intervals from the time of diagnosis until there was irreparable recurrence. Their time was extended so there was obviously something making a difference. This may be the psychneuroimmunologic (mind/body) approach to their disease.

This brings us back to the most important aspect of eliminating lung cancer and that is prevention. Society needs to make every effort to remove the causative factors that contribute to this disease. In addition to the use of tobacco products, there are other environmental issues that need to be addressed. These would include the use of toxic chemicals and asbestos in construction.

CHAPTER 13

OVARIAN CANCER

Ovarian carcinoma is a disease that has been around for a long time, but there may be some slow but steady progress in the number of cases diagnosed. There are probably environmental factors that are responsible for this increase such as high estrogen intake specifically and the use of pesticides.

One of the reasons many women take estrogen is because they have been told in the past that if they take estrogen they will look younger longer in the so-called 'forever young' syndrome. The first thing that happened when premarin, (a form of estrogen obtained from pregnant horse's urine), hit the market was that the manufacturers convinced women that prolonging youthful looks was one of the main reasons for taking it. There would be very few times that Warner would recommend taking Premarin unless he felt that the premenopausal symptoms of hot flashes and emotional instability was due to the lack of estrogen. There is an alternative estrogen therapy that might bring those symptoms under control.

This tumor spreads over the surface of the organ. It is not an invasive type of tumor. It is like the icing on a cake. It spreads over the outside surface of the abdominal contents and then where it touches the lining of the abdominal cavity it sets up an inflammatory reaction. The ovaries are hanging free in this cavity which is an open area. The body sends fluid to neutralize the poison or inflammatory reactions developing. Because of that, the patient accumulates a large amount of fluid in a hurry. Sometimes the patient becomes huge and as much as 2 or 3 or 4 gallons of fluid must be removed from the abdominal cavity.

Diagnosis of ovarian cancer is difficult and often is not detected until there is advanced tumor. It is often called the hidden tumor. There are some new things that have been helpful as diagnostic tools that pick up diseases earlier. If the doctor waits for the usual methods of diagnosis, it is often too late.

The most important method of diagnosis is through an annual pelvic examination that allows the doctor to get an idea of any ovarian enlargement or abnormality in that area. CA125, (a tumor marker), is commonly associated with most of the epithelial tumors of the ovary. CA125 is an antigen that comes from the surface of the tumor cell that can be picked up in the bloodstream and evaluate whether or not there is tumor present and whether that tumor is responding to the therapy that is being used. If it responds, then the level drops. If the CA125 is rising, the treatment is not successful or additional measures need to be added.

Tumors will arise mostly from the germinal or outer lining of the ovary. From these cells, the monthly deliverance of eggs to the vagina occurs so that during that certain time of the month a woman can become pregnant. If there is an abnormality in the growth of that follicle that produces the egg, then there can be the development of these epithelioid (ovarian) tumors. Because there are many types of ovarian tumors, there needs to be a pathologist's classification to determine the type. This classification does not determine growth potential or degree of malignancy.

The degree of malignancy does have some significance. It has more to do with how aggressive the doctor will be with the treatment program. If the tumor is not growing too rapidly, the physician does not have to be too aggressive. It usually develops in one ovary or the other. Ten percent will be in both sides. It grows in that one area on the surface and, giving cells off of it, spreads to the abdominal cavity. With the motion that is constantly going on in the abdominal cavity, there is a flow of tumor cells into all areas clear up under the diaphragm. This can cause irritation in the diaphragm and obstruction of lymphatic flow so that the first sign of the tumor would be the accumulation of fluid in the chest. The spread first of all is on the surface and usually travels all over until it adheres to the surface and gains a blood supply and starts to grow. It does not usually invade and normally does not spread into the lymph nodes or go to other parts of the body like other types of tumors do. If it does, it is usually a sign that there is a fairly large amount of tumor present and/or it has been there for quite awhile.

Diagnostic procedures determine what treatment program will be used. A CAT scan will reveal whether there are little nodules of tumor on the inside of the cavity or if they are producing obstruction some-place in the body. Also, this test will show whether the tumor has been there so long that the lymph nodes have become clogged with tumor and from that the patient is accumulating large amounts of fluid. The extent of the tumor needs to be known because if it is widespread a surgical procedure is not warranted. However, if the mass is localized, it can be removed.

*   *   *   *

Surgery may give the patient long-term control with a good quality of life. The disease is staged according to the amount of involvement.

Stage I: Limited to the ovary.

Stage 1 B: Present in both ovaries, but no fluid.

Stage 2: Fluid is present.

Stage 3: The tumor has begun to involve and adhere to other areas in the abdominal cavity.

Stage 4: The tumor has spread beyond the abdominal cavity and has a very poor prognosis.

*   *   *   *

In most cases, it is a surgical disease first. Surgery is a debulking procedure. The ovaries, the fallopian tubes and the uterus are removed because they are all intimately tied in with the ovarian cancer. There may be infiltrations in the tissues that surround these organs that will be removed when all of the pelvic organs are removed. Every time you treat this type of cancer, the patient is going to be sterilized and this is very difficult for younger women who lose their ability to reproduce.

It is very important that these psychological issues be dealt with because it's the patient's attitude that will help to determine how well she does with her illness. If she has a take charge attitude, she will feel there is hope and believe that she can contribute in a positive manner. It builds self-esteem and her body works more efficiently because of the mind/body relationship. If there is humor and happiness in her life and association with other people, she is going to feel much stronger and more able to keep her problems under control.

There may be times where there is so much tumor that the surgical procedure is not indicated because it is too difficult to get at the tumor. In such cases, in attempting to remove the tumor, the surgeon opens up the raw edges around the tumor. In this instance, as the healing occurs there is an open door for the tumor to go through and spread throughout the body disseminating the disease.

If the tumor is dealt with surgically, it does not necessarily take care of the problem because cancer is a systemic disease from its inception. The tumor can be removed thus decreasing the volume of tumor and if the immune system is strong enough then that could possibly be all the therapy needed and the patient will not have a recurrence. However, it is not possible for a tumor that has been sending off cells throughout the body for months before it gets symptomatic to have a surgical procedure that would be adequate. There would always be some tumor left behind.

It depends upon how rapidly it has grown and what the inciting factors are that make the tumor develop in the first place as to whether or not that tumor will be given enough impetus to grow and become a problem. Removing as much of the tumor as the surgeon can is essential and the hope is that the doctor may be able to use other things that will make the environment in the body unsuitable for any further progression of the tumor.

Hormone suppression is part of the therapy. When the surgeon removes the tumor, it may be possible in this day and age for the tumor to be put in a tumor bank and frozen with liquid nitrogen. Then it can be used later on if there is a relapse. With the improvement in our knowledge, the tumor can be unfrozen and it would be viable and suitable for making a vaccine for that particular patient. With the important progress in genetics, genetic alteration may eventually be possible to stop the growth of these abnormal cells. There are patients being treated now with this kind of therapy using a vaccine made from a pool of antigens collected from a large number of people with the same kind of illness.

When the surgeon operates, he will also remove the omentum, which is a pad of fat that hangs down like an apron over the abdominal contents. This is removed because it may have hidden tumor cells in it. It also makes it easier for certain types of treatment such as administering chemicals that are put into the peritoneal cavity and allowed to grow over the surface of the tumor and destroy it. There are special ways this can be done. A catheter can be inserted through the abdominal wall. Then chemical agents are squirted through this hollow tube into the peritoneal cavity. These agents then spread throughout the abdominal cavity and are taken up by the tumor cell to prevent it from growing. Many of the cytotoxic chemotherapy drugs can be used in this manner to prevent recurrence. It is especially important to do this after surgery in the hope of destroying circulating tumor cells that may have been spread by the surgical procedure.

* * * *

There are other treatments and the most successful treatment noted by Warner in the chemotherapy area was the use of one of the alkylating agents which is a derivative of the nitrogen mustard war gas. The patient takes this by mouth the first week of every month. It seems to be a way of dampening or suppressing the growth of the tumor cell without destroying the immune cell. The patient tolerates it well and has a good quality of life. Dr. Rutledge, head of gynecologic oncology at M.D. Anderson in Houston, Texas used that as a major form of therapy. His control rates were equal to, if not better then, many of the currently used treatment programs where high dose, very toxic drugs are used in an attempt to eradicate the tumor. It is not possible to use an agent that is not specific for tumor cells. In other words, it has to be taken up by the tumor cell to do any good. Any cell that is reproducing, be it normal or abnormal, takes up most chemotherapy drugs. So they have limited value.

It is known that there are a number of hormones that can be used. Tamoxifen, thought of mainly with breast cancer, can be used to prevent the uptake of hormones by the tumor cell. There are other agents such as progesterone that, in some people, in high doses, have been a good suppressant for the tumor cell. Articles have been written showing that there may be a stimulation if progesterone is used causing the tumor to grow more rapidly. These studies are incomplete at this time and Warner believed, given the advantages of the antibolic activity of progestinal agents, one of the normal female hormones, that such findings should be overlooked. The use of these agents can be beneficial as supplemental treatment in addition to conventional therapy.

*   *   *   *

X-ray treatment does not have any part to play in a treatment program because the amount of radiation therapy necessary to sterilize the abdominal cavity is more then normal tissues can accept. There is a great deal of damage to normal tissue when x-ray is used. It shrinks localized masses, relieves obstructions and stops bleeding so there are times it may be of temporary value, but it is limited in its effectiveness.

Warner believed his patients did better because of his attention to other areas that strengthen the immune system and improved the quality of their lives. He encouraged patients to strengthen the body. A diet of low sugar, low fat, high liquid, high fiber was very necessary in making a patient's immune system and general strength better. The patient's mind/body connections become an important factor in fighting this disease.

Warner believed it was possible to influence any malignancy favorably by taking care of the body. This means making your body stronger and stimulating the immune system through specific vitamins, minerals and diet. This influences the course of the illness. Healing occurs because we make the healing come from inside out. It is not necessarily the things the physicians do.

The doctor can help buy time, but it is what the patient's body does in day to day activities that will determine whether or not that person is going to keep the tumor under control. Warner spent a lot of time finding ways he could make the patient stronger. He sometimes used male hormones in some forms like the anabolic steroids to stimulate the appetite, stimulate the bone marrow, and build up muscular strength so the patient could tolerate exercising better. Exercise burns up materials secreted by the tumor that are poisonous to the body and contribute to feeling ill with symptoms of the disease.

There are exercises of all types. The patient can start with the yoga type exercises where muscles are gently stretched and pulled to the full extent of their range of motion. Yoga is done in a quiet, relaxing atmosphere even using meditation and music to help the patient relax. This contributes to building a good mental attitude toward the disease. This may be very important especially in tumors that seem to be endrocine sensitive, such as breast and thyroid in addition to ovaries.

Tumors are stimulated one way or another by the hormone environment. If the patient does all these extra things, the body becomes stronger and tolerates the cancer better. Also, adequate rest is recommended to recharge a patient's batteries so the immune system will work better. The patient needs to learn how to breathe deeply to get better oxygenation and use anti-oxidant medication.

As far as new therapies are concerned, vaccines are going to be an important way to treat. There is also evidence that antibodies can be used. These antibodies are made and incubated from the tumor cell. They are specific for the tumor cell so that when injected back into that patient it will kill the tumor. That is a promising area that needs more investigation. There are other agents that can be injected in an attempt to control the disease, but that is still in the future. With the speed with which things are changing now, it probably won't be too long until many of these new possibilities will be readily available to any patient under the care of a qualified oncologist.

*   *   *   *

Most of the time Warner would get patients who had been told by their doctor that there was nothing more they could do for them. They were told to go home and get their affairs in order. Or they were people who had been told by their doctor that the recommended therapy was probably not going to work, it was going to be very toxic, but the doctor still recommended that they try it. Given the extreme negativity of this approach, the patient usually turned it down and came to him. So he often did get patients late in the course of their illness. It was amazing to him that he saw people in all stages of that particular illness that became long term survivors using many different approaches.

The common denominator here was that the patient was a take charge person and tried to learn about her illness. With attitudinal adjustments they were able to strengthen the immune system, had a happy existence, learned to live with the illness and were able to keep the disease under control. That seemed to be the secret of the success of these individuals.

Warner had many patients who have been living a long time. One patient had Stage IV ovarian cancer and was told by her doctor that she had six weeks to live. Her husband was very diligent and worked hard to find a treatment program that would be acceptable to her and would promise a different outcome. He talked to other people, heard about Warner's program and, fortunately, she became his patient. It has been twenty-five years since her original diagnosis and she has had no further difficulty. She had surgery but no chemotherapy or radiation treatment. She was given BCG, hormone therapy, dietary and other supportive measures. She is a long-term survivor who has been extremely well except as she has grown older she has had problems with arteriosclerosis, a small stroke, and that has interfered with her quality of life.

We had another young lady who in mid-life had to have treatment. She consulted with many different doctors before she selected Warner. She decided that his approach was the one she wanted. Hormones, BCG and interferon were used and she is living and well fifteen years since she started treatment. She had invasive tumor outside the ovaries when she was diagnosed, but has never had a relapse.

CHAPTER 14

COLON CANCER

The main thing to know about colon tumors is that they are the second lowest prevalent tumor that occurs in humans. It is a disease that is generally recognized to be due to nutrition errors. In other words, you are eating the wrong things or eating foods that will raise the cortisone and sugar levels. These and other factors come together to give a person colon cancer.

The typical colon cancer producing diet is poly saturated fats—any of the fats that are cooked—the hydrogenated fats specifically and fried foods. These change the fat from an unsaturated state to a saturated. This means that all the radicals in the molecules of fat have been changed to ones that are solid. Then fat lipid plaques are formed in various parts of the body that lead to the ultimate damage as the result of the excess fat. In addition to diet, it is known that Vitamin E and C protect the passage of material inside the cell where they hit the DNA.

What is needed is to cut down the abnormal oxidation, the absorption of toxic materials that damage the cells and this is accomplished with a high fiber diet. The fiber may serve as a substance that promotes rapid expulsion. It could be material that adheres to the fibers or there could be materials in the fibers that cause phytic acid that needs to be neutralized. These are the agents that are needed to neutralize the oxygen, the free radicals and the anti-oxidant effect. Then the patient needs to make sure the diet is free of other substances like sugars that are cancer promoting.

As we grow older, specifically from about age 45 on, there comes a time when the body does not repair itself as rapidly as it should. It may be that the body has been overstressed or the individual has not been getting the right amount of rest, exercise, and the proper diet as mentioned. Therefore, the colon is strained and stressed. It is not as strong as it should be and that makes the damage of certain food materials even greater in some people. It can cause accelerated aging or promote the development of chronic diseases.

The number one thing that would make the doctor suspect colon cancer in a patient is usually a change in bowel habits. This would be a slowing down of the number and frequency of stools and also the contour of the stools changing from ones that are normal size to long stringy stools. Then there may be some color changes usually indicative of microscopic bleeding. The stool darkens from a dark gray to black. The normal color is brown. This symptom indicates a more advanced state of the problem. 80 to 90 per cent of all colon tumors are secondary to diet or other things we put in our bodies that keep it from working the way it should.

* * * *

In making a diagnosis, the main thing was the initial laboratory studies. As mentioned, the first thing that would be present was a low-grade microscopic type of bleeding. The patient usually would be moderately anemic. For a long time, people thought that irrespective of dietary changes, colon cancer was hereditary, but that is not the case. There have been extensive studies done and genetic factors have been pretty well determined in the specimens examined. More proof is needed on how genetic factors and dietary changes interact. People are not going to quit eating a certain way unless it can actually be proven that there is a disadvantage to continuing with an unhealthy diet.

One of the best ways is to check for colon cancer is the patient's stool with the occult blood test. This is a small postage stamp size square that has been impregnated with material including the PSA and other antigens to see if there is any bleeding. The bleeding will be manifested by a tiny color change and that means there is excess bleeding in the GI tract. At the current time, the presence of occult blood and change in stool habits are the most important factors. There may be additional signs when the patient suddenly develops intestinal obstruction. This happens when a person doesn't pay very much attention to his body. This person suddenly sees that they have put on a lot of weight, his abdominal girth has increased and shortness of breath becomes a common problem. Unfortunately, when these symptoms occur, the individual often rationalizes and does not follow up like he should. It is interesting that if there is a drive with free testing more people will take advantage of that. A fair number of people will be found to have polyps or some of the other symptoms that if continued in its current cycle will result in the development of malignant tumor.

When it had been determined that the patient had colon cancer, Warner recommended surgery to remove as much of the volume of tumor as possible. If the growth pattern is not stopped, which is the circumferential growth around the inside of the bowel wall, it will eventually get big enough to occlude the opening so that nothing comes through. To wait for radiation, chemotherapy, other drugs or hormone treatments to help the patient usually takes a period of three to six months before making any significant difference and that is too long to wait.

After surgery, the tumor markers were analyzed to see if there was an elevation of the CEA. The physician needed to check to see if there was some hidden or occult bleeding over time and if the patient was anemic because of it. That is one of the initial symptoms and needs to be treated appropriately immediately. The treatment for anemia is not transfusions, but it was necessary to make the diagnosis as to why the patient has anemia. What are the specific reasons that the body is not responding to the tumor antigen by manufacturing a substance of its own that will counteract and spontaneously cause the blood count to rise?

Warner believed that if colon cancer is detected early and he and the patient did certain things, it was one of the more curable cancers. In order for this to be possible, the patient must really take responsibility for his health. This means making the necessary lifestyle changes in order to stay healthy.

CHAPTER 15

SOFT TISSUE CANCER

These are tumors that arise from the muscles, tendons, and the supporting structures of the body; those not actively involved in metabolic activity in the body. If you divide the body into the cell of origin of the various organs, you find that there are cells that line the body cavities and various organs like the liver, kidneys and lungs. These are derived from one series of cells that are formed in a certain position in the early embryo. It will become the inside cell sandwiched between the cells that eventually become the muscles, bones, joints, and nerves. These tissues are the supporting structures of the body making it possible for the body to work in a coordinated way. The tumors that develop are sarcoma cancers as differentiated from carcinomas.

Cancers of the muscles are fairly rare compared to other types of cancer or carcinomas; probably 10% of all malignant tumors. They develop in the muscles that arise within the organs themselves like fiber sarcomas that develop in the stomach. It is not stomach cancer but a fiber sarcoma.

If the tumor is slow in developing and gets to the point where the lesion is big enough to produce symptoms, the patient is then going to have an indication that there is a problem in an area that has to do with motion. In other words, the patient gets painful nodules or masses on bones, joints or some organ of the body that is made worse by activity.

These tumors develop from muscle tissue, bone, tendon, fat or any of the supporting structures that hold the body together or serve as the suppliers of nerve, lymphatics or blood to various parts of the body. They all have a metabolic function.

There are soft tissue carcinomas that arise from fat cells, tendons, muscles and nerves. They usually develop first as an aching nodule that interferes with running or some particular activity. It rarely causes any incapacitating symptom unless it is in a special area where it serves as an obstruction or it develops from a nerve and the nerve stimulates pain because of the presence of the tumor.

Most of the tumors actually are a variance of fibra sarcomas from the fibrous tissue in an area that has been irritated for a period of years until it starts to grow independently, and then interferes with function at that point. As it gets bigger, it may spread into contiguous areas, but that type of spread makes it easier for the surgeon to remove the muscle bundle or the area from which the tumor arises. In this case, the surgeon has an excellent chance of removing the major part of the tumor. The prognosis is good if treated early and adequately.

$$* \qquad * \qquad * \qquad *$$

In diagnosis, the main thing to find out was what kind of tumor the patient had and the extent of the tumor. This was accomplished by a biopsy of the tumor to get the cell type and to determine if there is a body reaction against the tumor. What was the body doing against that tumor? If the body was infiltrating it with certain cells that would be an indication that the body was trying to get rid of it.

The surgical approach as the number one approach in treatment was predicated on what was found with the diagnostic procedures. These procedures were the CAT scan and perhaps a bone scan to determine whether or not there was any growth extending into the adjacent bone. A chest x-ray was necessary to be sure the tumor had not been present long enough to spread to other parts of the body such as metastatic disease in the lung and the liver. This can occur early on with these type tumors, but because they grow slowly there was an excellent chance of removing it while it was still a localized problem. Blood studies could be done, but there were no tumor markers readily available at the time.

Warner usually recommended surgery to remove the tumor. The main job of the surgeon was to be sure he got all around the tumor and removed the full extent of it. If it developed in a muscle, then that muscle was removed from the insertion of the muscle to a distant area or the origin of the muscle where it would be in one of the approximate bone areas. This was the best first approach. The surgeon could operate and then wait until it recurred and if it was the usual, average soft tissue carcinoma, it would take 3, 4, to 5 years before it came back. When it did recur, the surgeon might be able to do the same operation again with good results.

Some medical practitioners gave radiation therapy after surgery, but the effectiveness of this therapy was doubtful. It was not known whether radiation would kill off a number of cells in the area of the primary tumor. If the patient had just a few tumor cells remaining then there was the possibility that radiation would be an effective agent. However, if there was a large amount of tumor, the amount of radiation necessary to sterilize the entire tumor cell was more than what the adjacent lung tissue or other body tissues would tolerate. If it was in the extremity, it was not so bad because most of those tissues are much more tolerant of radiation. Radiation treatment used for a tumor that develops from muscle that was deep within the abdomen or in the back goes through both normal and abnormal tissues in the back as it passes through the body and could damage the normal tissues to a great extent.

Whatever treatment was used, it was necessary to reduce the volume of tumor first. As with tumors in any other areas, it was necessary to strengthen the body's response mechanism and the immune system before reducing the volume of tumor. Diagnostic procedures must be completed to show where the cancer was located before any surgical approach.

Perhaps the main procedure was using the tumor bank again, putting the tumor in liquid nitrogen and saving it if it was in an area where the tumor can be saved for several years. Eventually, ways may become available to use that tumor to make an individual vaccine for the patient. There are other studies not quite ready which, when they become available, will make it possible to use part of the saved tumor to make treatment programs that would be effective in controlling the tumor.

Chemotherapy is another option. However, the cytotoxic drugs have not been too successful because there are not that many cells in a growth phase at any one time. So the amount of cellular destruction that occurs with the cytotoxic drugs is not very large. It takes a long time before you can sterilize the majority of the cells with the drugs that will stop its reproductive capacity.

Warner did not use chemotherapy because he believed it was not a particularly effective way of treatment because of the lack of specificity. This was true except where there were some tumors such as the germ cell tumors and testicular tumors that would respond dramatically to chemotherapy

Some tumors grew so rapidly that there was no other way to keep up with them, such as the leukemias. The turnover rate is so rapid that there is nothing that will control the overgrowth. If it was allowed to continue, it would snuff out the normal function of a particular organ or a system in the body producing a condition that is incompatible with life. For this reason, chemotherapy was used in rapidly growing, very aggressive tumors. However, it was possible to counteract this rapid growth without using the cytotoxic drugs. Interferons and interleukins could be used in treating certain types of leukemia and were becoming more effective.

One of the most intriguing things about soft tissue sarcomas was the large number of people who did very well with long term control of their illness with a good quality of life. They achieved this without going through disfiguring surgical procedures or the very severe cytotoxic therapies that are often offered

*   *   *   *

Warner had a patient named Ralph (name changed) whose problem began with pain in his hip and the problem was not helped with radiation. The tumor continued to grow and was extending into the tissues about the pelvis so an extensive surgical procedure was performed during which a portion of the hip bone, all of the hip joint, and the upper portion of the femur were removed.

Ralph had to have a very large, cumbersome prosthesis made in order to get around, but Ralph was determined that he would be able to support his wife and continue on in his job. Unfortunately, he was fired because he had cancer and had to find other employment. He took the necessary courses for a real estate license and became reasonably successful at it. He was fully ambulatory and had a good quality of life. He's alive and doing well today which is pushing the 25 to 30 year level. Aggressive treatments were not used after the surgery.

Warner said that he did spend a great deal of time with Ralph helping him to develop a positive attitude. He showed him how to take charge of his illness and encouraged him to change professions and get into something he liked and could do. Immune stimulation using BCG vaccine, and lavamisole to increase his lymphocyte level were used. Large amounts of vitamins and some minerals were recommended, but no particular herbal medications were given. Ralph has done extremely well with a very conservative program. Some people would say there was no therapy except for the extensive surgery.

Other people have had this surgery, but they did not have the good attitude and work as hard as Ralph did. They did not change their lifestyle and they allowed themselves to continue in a feeling of depression, which lowers their immunity. Therefore, they became victims of their disease. In Ralph's case, he rallied and overcame it. The surgery was necessary but the other collateral things he did contributed to his long-term survival. The surgery reduced the volume of tumor below a point that his body was better able to handle it, which may be one explanation. Before surgery, the x-rays showed penetration beyond the areas of the bones and the joints and into the soft tissues around the area, indicating that this was a Stage III tumor that was out of control.

*   *   *   *

Warner had a number of other similar cases. There was a very beautiful lady who was in her early forties. He first saw her when she was in Junior High School. She had a severe lesion in her knee. Other doctors had tried to resect it and she had been given radiation, which was not successful. Non-specific immune stimulation was used and she changed her lifestyle. She did not do all the things Warner recommended at first. He wanted her to have an amputation because the distortion of the leg was so bad it twisted her spine and she walked in a very peculiar way. Often, when she was tired, she had to use a crutch. The tumor grew out through the skin of the knee. She had severe radiation damage because the amount of radiation given was greater then normal tissues would tolerate and it produced radiation necrosis. But that was done on the basis that her leg was going to be taken off anyway. However, after the radiation, she refused to have the amputation and, as a result, she went along for a number of years with the problem and distortion that is seen with these kinds of lesions.

She was finally convinced to have the amputation and a prosthesis and she did extremely well with that. She is a beautiful woman, a model type, very stunning. She walks well with a slight limp, which is hardly noticeable, and her back straightened up. It was just through attitude, working at it, making her body stronger and strengthening her immune system that she was able to do so well.

*   *   *   *

Another individual had a chondro sarcoma of the knee and he, too, did not have conventional therapy, but had non-specific immune therapy. It really was very non-specific because there were not any treatments that would make any big difference. He is still doing very well and it is now 35 years or so since he was first diagnosed. His previous job was as a service station operator. Now he has some supervisory jobs and does not have to be as physically active.

*   *   *   *

There was a patient who was a nurse and she worked over nine years following her treatment for chondro sarcoma. Her treatment involved hormone therapy to keep up her general body strength and appetite and she worked hard on her attitude and other positive lifestyle changes. As long as Warner was in charge of her illness, she did very well. Then she moved away and the doctors in the other city decided there was no reason this patient was responding so well to the medicines prescribed by Warner and discontinued them. It wasn't very long before she began to have metastatic disease in the lungs. She then had a recurrence in the knee and died from her disease. During the 9 or 10 years she was Warner's patient, she had no evidence of problems and continued working.

*   *   *   *

There was another young lady who had a sarcoma of the thigh twenty years ago. It was irradiated and the part of the bone that contained the tumor was resected. The surgery was extensive and a rod was inserted from the hip to the knee, which substituted for the bone. She bicycles, works as a teller in a bank on a regular basis, has had two children and a good quality of life without any medications.

There were a number of other patients with carcinogenic sarcomas that are still doing well as far as is known. Those patients have been able to do remarkable things. One young man who had his leg amputated went on into the finals of the handicapped Olympic Games and won some medals there as a skier.

*   *   *   *

Another young girl was a cyclist, swimmer and dancer. She had to have her hip joint removed and that portion of the adjacent pelvic bone. Her prosthesis resembled a little shelf that she sat on. It was contoured to resemble the pelvic bone structure. An artificial leg was added to the prosthesis and she became very adept at using it. She was very proud of what she had done. Her personality blossomed under treatment because her self-esteem was restored. She demonstrated to herself in her disease control that she was capable of doing remarkable things. This always makes a person stronger. Warner believed the physician's role was to assist in the process of healing.

The physician can help the patient buy a little bit of time until the immune system gets strong enough to correct the genetic or chemical abnormalities that have developed in the body and leads to the overgrowth of these cells and their lack of body control. This patient did not have any further treatment. She did not want to be reminded of the fact that she had a problem. No one is available now that will look at her from the standpoint of possible psychosomatic complaints and the physiologic support system that she needs through psychoneuroimmunology. All of this has been important in how well she handled her illness.

*   *   *   *

All of these patients came to Warner during the initial stages of their disease so he was able to recommend the treatments, including surgery, from the beginning. His treatment approach was initially conventional followed by supportive measures such as vitamins, counseling and lifestyle changes. He did the supportive therapy before definitive therapy was started.

He used various kinds of non-specific vaccines that stimulated the immune system. His feeling was that if the immune system was stimulated in one spot or under one circumstance, the whole immune system reacted to a certain degree. Some parts may react very strongly and, therefore, the patient is helped a great deal by non-specific vaccines. In others, there is not too much change that can be measured. His goal was to make sure the patient was as strong as possible before using any other treatments.

Warner's long experience in treating soft tissue carcinomas was such that he believed if the type of treatment discussed here was used more often there would be a significant number of people living longer then those who have only conventional therapy. He believed that this was undoubtedly true in all types of tumors, but it was especially striking to him in the soft tissue sarcomas.

CHAPTER 16

GENERAL COMMENTS ON DIAGNOSIS AND TREATMENT

There is a need for a classification that puts emphasis on the staging of cancer. That is, how far and how extensive the tumor has grown. Physicians are seeing lesions earlier and earlier. If the patient is in the early stages of the disease, it may be possible to stimulate the body and the immune system and have the patient work at being well and completely reversing the disease process. In some situations, as in the breast, there is a tendency for some doctors to treat a nonmalignant condition as a malignant condition and do aggressive therapy. Then they say the improvement is due to the aggressive therapy when in reality the tumor had not really progressed into the invasive, infiltrating, malignant phase of the growth pattern.

There are cases where women have had their breast removed even though they had no cancer because of cancer in their mother, sisters or relatives. This is a real problem. A number of women came to Warner who were in turmoil. They had been advised by a surgeon to have a mastectomy. Sometimes the oncologist would agree with the surgeon. Just as often, the oncologist would say they should be having radiation treatment or surgery and they also should have chemotherapy in addition to the other procedures. These are drastic treatments.

Many doctors are looking so hard at treating the disease and not enough at the patient and circumstances that might contribute to the development of this illness. This illness is really a reaction to injury that occurs due to repetitive injury that occurs over a period of years. That injury can be psychological, emotional or spiritual. It does not have to be physical or chemical.

The question of whether amputation of the breast because of cancer in the family cannot be answered in this day and age. The proper studies have not been done to show that the patients do better then when they are empowered to fight any possible illness. They can be instructed how this is possible if the tools they have within their own body are used. Until that is done and compared with conventional therapy, you cannot say that one is better than the other.

There are many women who have refused to have mammograms. They have refused to have follow-up therapies that are advised by their doctor and are living and well many years later. There is a need to know how many people are doing well years later compared to the treatment they received. It could be very surprising to learn how many people can live a long time with a minimal amount of treatment. It may be treatments we do not understand or agree with, but at least it was the right one for the patient who had faith in it and as a result of that faith was able to overcome his illness. These are essential things that need to be studied. Oncologists need to know whenever there has been successful control of the cancer patient. Successes are not studied. Failures are studied and, therefore, doctors become committed to failure. Warner believed that most doctors were not doing the therapies that would enable them to do the most for the patient.

Doctors have wonderful techniques to detect suspicious lesions at a very early stage before they become infiltrating or invasive. However, then the patient can be converted into a cripple because of the fear regarding the possibility of cancer. Because the patient is fearful of a very poor, dire outcome, he lives in a constant state of fear. All of this contributes to immune suppression.

*   *   *   *

It is impossible to outline what should be done for every type cancer. There is no cookbook approach that will apply to every patient. Each patient needs to have an individualized treatment program. In every major tumor situation in the body, there are instances where people have done well when they have taken charge of their illness. This occurs when they have a program that fits their beliefs and gives them the opportunity to take charge in the decision making that goes into their treatment regimen.

Warner said that new agents, which are immunologic manifestations of the wonderful defense mechanism in our bodies, are helping physicians learn to overcome a wide variety of illnesses. Whether it is multiple sclerosis, lupus, kidney, thyroid diseases, arthritis, cancer, they are all immune deficiency diseases. Everyone needs to concentrate on taking care of the immune system. Our body does have the capacity to make a big difference in whatever illness we have if we can make the environment within our body as hostile as possible for tumor cell growth. This is accomplished by making sure that everything we do is dedicated to wellness. The more that is learned about using our own defense mechanisms, the stronger we will become.

Warner believed that the future of cancer therapy would be undergoing massive changes eventually. More honesty is needed in the approach to diagnosis and treatment. In other words, doctors need to look at what treatments are being used and the results of chosen therapy. Are significant inroads being made by continuing on the present course while neglecting the individual with the disease? The therapies offered need to be tested from a wide variety of approaches. If patients showed improvement, it was necessary to keep track of those individuals. With this approach, doctors would gain knowledge about what could be added to the treatment program that would favorably influence the final outcome. Are significant inroads being made by continuing on the present course, which is taking care of the disease while neglecting the individual with the disease?

*   *   *   *

Due to earlier and improved diagnosis, Warner began to see patients whose disease was not as far advanced. Also, there were more people working on cancer and cancer problems then ever before. He noticed that he was not seeing cases that had been growing rampantly over a period of years without any medical attention. When patients were seen in the earlier stages of their disease it was possible to make a difference.

Some disease situations seem to resolve spontaneously. Warner did not think that there is such a thing as spontaneous remission. Spontaneous remission occurs when the immune system is suddenly stimulated in such a way that it kicks in and its defense mechanisms are so powerful that they destroy the tumor. That is a favorable response of the immune system. It is not a spontaneous reduction for which there is no explanation.

There were many times when Warner felt as if he was a voice crying in the wilderness in view of the opposition to his philosophy and treatment program. He knew that it was possible to concentrate on a variety of treatments because there are substances available for treatment that are the same as the body manufactures to kill abnormal cells. Our bodies do have mechanisms to keep us free of disease. Because we have these kinds of mechanisms, it is possible to significantly improve the course of a patient's illness.

The mind/body psychological aspects were important in Warner's treatment. The medical community is becoming more aware of the possibilities and probabilities of this kind of therapy. He believed that far less time should be spent on the rat and mouse game in order to make greater and faster progress. In other words, research should not be spending time learning the effect on animals because there is not a complementary action or reaction in the human. Therefore, the information obtained is not very valuable.

If the patient was willing to participate in a program that includes the mind/body aspect, it was possible to measure the beneficial effects of this approach. The idea of saying that the doctor can only use new ideas after a patient has been given the maximum surgery, radiation and chemotherapy is ridiculous. This approach does everything possible to beat the patient down and practically kill him by destroying his immune system. This approach believes in exhausting every other type of treatment, then giving the patients something to stimulate their immune system. These stimuli are not that strong. They are not huge, powerful agents like some of the antibiotics. Therefore, the immune system is overwhelmed. If immune stimulants were given before more aggressive treatment, it would make it easier for the immune cells to work against tumor.

CHAPTER 17

DECISIONS ON TREATMENT

The major reason so little progress has been made in solving the cancer problem is that there is no adequate agency for collecting data. It would seem reasonable to assume that every cancer patient is reported with a follow-up on treatment used and the success or failure of such treatment. Only by shared knowledge will the most effective therapies ever be revealed.

When I requested statistics on cancer treatments and survival from the National Institutes of Health, I was amazed at the worthless information I received. Their report was based on data gathered from three hospitals in the United States and then extrapolated to give figures on incidence of each type of cancer. It was like a Gallup poll for cancer. It seems that no one has any idea of exactly how many people are diagnosed with cancer or what treatments are effective. *It should be required by law that every single diagnosis of cancer is reported with follow-up on treatment and survival and the information made available to every cancer specialist.*

Here in the State of Washington, a Cancer Registry was finally established by law in 1991 and funded in 1992. The collecting agencies are the Fred Hutchinson Cancer Research Center (FHCRC) and Blue Mountain Oncology in Walla Walla, Washington. This is a step in the right direction. Every cancer patient must now be reported to the

Cancer Registry. Unfortunately, there is no follow-up on treatment and survival rates.

In 1984, the FHCRC was awarded a grant from the National Institutes of Health to do an ongoing statistical study on cancer patients and their treatments. Most of their information was provided by hospitals. Glenn Warner was the only oncologist in private practice that opened his medical records to this study. He was interested in having his therapies compared to the so-called conventional treatments. The statisticians who worked on his records were impressed with the meticulous and thorough records he kept on each patient.

In spite of unfounded criticism over the years that the medical community did not know what treatments he was using, that information is all on record. However, as far as I know, there has never been a comprehensive study published making a comparison between conventional therapies (radiation and chemotherapy) and the immunotherapy approach used by Warner.

One early release did show that Warner's patients did as well as, if not better than, patients receiving other treatments, especially those being treated for melanoma. However, in this early statistical analysis, all of his long term survival patients were eliminated. This certainly skewed the results. Another factor that was not measured was quality of life. Instead of being ill from treatment, Warner's patients had virtually no side effects.

*   *   *   *

Recently, there was a rather amazing article by Yochi Dreazen of the Knight Ridder newspapers titled, "What's Next Once Cancer is Cured?" I read the article with amazement. Millions of people are suffering and dying of this frightening disease today and the author is worrying about the impact on the nation's economic status, demographic make-up and behavioral patterns. The author says that curing cancer would save billions of dollars in lost productivity and treatment costs each year, but it would also increase life expectancy putting new strains on the Social Security system. And what about all those doctors, health professionals, pharmaceutical companies and research scientists whose entire livelihood is fueled by the suffering of cancer patients? Cancer is a huge industry and yet I never expected to see such an opinion in print.

In the article, Dr. Henry Aaron, a health economist at the Brookings Institute, a Washington think tank, is quoted as saying that curing cancer, "simply means postponing death and allowing someone to die from some other cause, which might be more or less expensive than cancer." Dreazen suggests that there would be a serious downsizing of the medical profession if there were not cancer patients to take care of. If we carry this author's opinion a step further, why try to cure heart disease or any other life-threatening illness?

I do not believe that Dreazen would feel the same way if he were the one diagnosed with cancer. Like the rest of us, he would want all the resources available to survive this disease.

*   *   *   *

So what do we do? Initially, we want to believe that our oncologist is knowledgeable about all the latest developments in cancer therapies. I have learned that this is not necessarily true.

We need to take a step back and consider our options. Our cancer has been developing for a long time and we should not rush into any treatment program. There are many resources available and we need to do our own research. When we are sufficiently informed, we need to ask our doctor questions. If he is not amenable to this, find another oncologist. The patient/physician relationship is of primary importance to our recovery and we need a professional who welcomes our imput.

Obtain a second opinion. One patient I know personally who was diagnosed with ovarian cancer interviewed seven doctors, which most of us might consider excessive. Six out of the seven recommended chemotherapy after surgery. Glenn Warner was the only one who suggested a different approach—one that would build her immune system along with lifestyle changes. Warner's approach appealed to her and she is alive and well many years later. An interesting sidelight to her quest is that she asked each doctor she consulted to give her the names of five patients who had survived his recommended treatment for at least five years. Warner was the only doctor who was willing to provide her with this information.

Accept the diagnosis but not the verdict. I wish doctors would not tell patients that, in their opinion, they have x number of months or years to live. More than anything we need to have HOPE. Our doctor should not minimize the seriousness of our illness, but should give us hope that working together we can win this battle.

Be proactive. Become involved in our recovery by changing whatever we can to improve our health. We can change to a healthier diet, exercise and improve our mental health by learning to deal with stress and confronting problems in relationships.

Work toward *spiritual renewal.* There is great comfort in believing in a power greater than ourselves. We can increase our connection to a loving God by reading, praying and connecting with those people who will help in our growth.

After we have made a decision on the therapy we want, we need to have the *courage* to follow through. We need to believe wholeheartedly in the path we have chosen and surround ourselves with positive people. It is a confusing time fraught with anxiety and we need to come to a time when we are at peace with our decisions. We are in charge of our health and well being and the doctor we choose should be the facilitator, working with us to achieve our goals.

As a long time survivor of metastatic cancer, I am a strong advocate of a healthy lifestyle. I believe the American public is waking up to the fact that each individual is responsible for about 90% of their health. As more and more people become aware of the advantages of positive lifestyle changes, they are not going to passively accept anything the doctor tells them. In fact, they are going to search for the doctor that will enter into a partnership with them, a doctor who will give them hope and the quality of life they desire as they work together to conquer their cancer. Even better, as the public becomes better informed, they will adopt a lifestyle that will prevent cancer.

CHAPTER 18

SUCCESS STORIES

In the eventual persecution of Dr. Warner, the Medical Disciplinary Board (later changed to Medical Quality Assurance Commission) never listened to any of the hundreds of patients under the care of this fine physician. The following are excerpts from some of the hundreds of letters to the MQAC (which the Board refused to read) in the outpouring of support and pleadings for him to continue their treatments.

Their letters speak eloquently of Warner's success in the treatment of his patients. These are knowledgeable, intelligent individuals who made a choice in their cancer therapy. You will see that many of them had already failed the conventional therapies of radiation and chemotherapy. Contrary to the belief of the MQAC that they needed to be protected, these patients wanted the right to make their own decisions.

*   *   *   *

"When patients are faced with life-threatening illnesses for which the medical profession has no certain cures—e.g. cancer or AIDS—they should not be deprived of access to alternative forms of treatment offered by qualified medical doctors. The continuing harassment of Dr. Glenn Warner by the Medical Disciplinary Board is insulting to him and also to cancer victims who make thoughtful, informed choices about how they wish to spend what may be the final months of their lives.

"The standard treatments administered to cancer patients—-surgery, chemotherapy and radiation—-are painful, invasive, damaging to the patient's immune system, and often horrendously expensive. These treatments also are ineffective in the vast majority of cases. Over the course of my 69 years, I have watched countless relatives, friends, colleagues and acquaintances die from cancer, usually after months or years of gruesome medical treatment.

"Given the dismal statistics of existing cancer treatments, patients should have alternatives available to them while being under the general oversight of a medical doctor. When I decided not to undergo the extreme treatment program proposed to me in 1984 by a cancer surgeon (who gave me a 25 percent chance of surviving 5 years) at the Virginia Mason Clinic—-radical facial, mouth and neck surgery, followed by radiation and chemotherapy—-it was because I did not choose to spend months or years in and out of the hospital suffering the combined effects of surgery, chemotherapy and radiation. I also did not choose to be forced into early retirement by crippling and disfiguring facial and neck surgery.

"Instead, I sought a more moderate form of treatment and was fortunate enough to find Dr. Warner who used radiation therapy combined with other treatments designed to strengthen my immune system. Six months after I started treatment with Dr. Warner, in March 1985, a second CAT-scan showed no sign of cancer and I have never had a recurrence.

"Over a long career, Dr. Warner has trained in a number of medical specialties (oncology, cancer surgery, pathology, radiation and immunotherapy) and throughout his career he has kept abreast of new developments in oncology. His patients benefit from his long experience and comprehensive up-to-date knowledge. For example, one of the vaccines he used in treating me in 1984-5 was BCG, a tuberculosis vaccine known to attack tumors in humans. A few years later, in 1990, specialists in bladder cancer began using BCG after a National Cancer

Institute trial showed that '74 percent of patients with bladder carcinoma in situ responded to the treatment as against 42 percent for those using the established cancer drug adriamycin', according to the Wall Street Journal of May 22, 1990. Ironically, many of the so-called 'experimental' cancer treatments, in fact, represent state-of-the-art medicine.

"Similarly, Dr. Warner has long advocated that his patients follow a low-fat, high fiber diet, the type of diet now recognized as beneficial for the maintenance of health and prevention of disease. His overall treatment strategy is designed to improve the patient's physical and mental health and strengthen the immune system while the cancer is being treated. He also does everything possible to maintain his patient's quality of life while they are undergoing treatment. Most patients are concerned about the effects of the disease and invasive cancer treatments on their own lives and the lives of their families, yet most oncologists pay scant attention to this concern.

"I have accumulated several large files of recent periodical articles about new developments in the understanding and treatment of cancer, all of which confirm Dr. Warner's general approach to cancer treatment. I can only conclude that the individuals who criticize him are ignorant of these developments or are motivated by professional jealousy or greed. They should be learning from his successes, for as more is known about cancer, Dr. Warner's work will be vindicated I believe. His critics will be the ones who look foolish, and so will the Medical Disciplinary Board if it continues to acquiesce to their complaints. The Board should listen to Dr. Warner's patients and protect our right to the outstanding medical treatment he has provided and continues to provide us." M.G., Ph.D.

*   *   *   *

"I am writing to you regarding the pending hearing and threatened disciplinary actions against Dr. Glenn Warner of Northwest Oncology Clinic, Seattle.

"I have been a patient of Dr. Warner's since August 1987 when, after a biopsy performed at Overlake Hospital, I was diagnosed as having breast cancer. For several years, I had had fibrous breast disease, but nobody had suggested a mammogram until a few months before the cancer was found. In June and July, my family doctor had even prescribed estrogen for symptoms of menopause!

"After the biopsy, I was advised, without further tests and/or second opinion, to have a modified radical mastectomy with removal of all axillary lymph nodes. This procedure was scheduled for two days after the biopsy. I was also told that chemotherapy was to follow if the lymph nodes were positive.

"After I recovered from the first shock, I listened to concerned family members and knowledgeable friends who referred me to other health care institutions, both 'main line' and for alternative treatment, to support groups and recovered cancer patients. I canceled the surgery and embarked on a crash course in what cancer is and what treatments are currently available.

"Dr. Warner was one of the physicians I visited. After an initial examination, he outlined my condition and the suggested treatment: lumpectomy with node sampling, followed by radiation. He was the first physician to counsel my husband and children; he did this in a thorough and caring manner. For the first time since the diagnosis, we all saw a light at the end of the tunnel.

"By that time, I realized that this was the medical expertise coupled with genuine care and total dedication to the welfare of the patient that I was looking for in a physician. The treatment suggested by Dr. Warner was good common sense practice. Where it differed was that he was offering care of the whole person, never dictating what had to be done, but letting me choose and participate. This gave me a sense of control which, I subsequently learned, is all-important for recovery. Therefore, after the lumpectomy, carried out by a surgeon of my own choosing, and the following radiation, I availed myself of the possibilities for long-term control of my disease. I received physical therapy, changed my nutrition under the guidance of a nutritionist, embarked on a fitness program and underwent psychological counseling for a short while and courses in guided imagery.

"From the start, I felt physically well, able to remain active and working. Psychologically, my determination to recover was constantly reinforced and supported by Dr. Warner and his staff. I had been through medical problems prior to this bout with cancer, but I had never before felt to this degree that I can be in charge, that I can actively participate in regaining and keeping my good health. The quality of my life has improved overall, as has my general health, and my mental outlook has never been better.

"I have learned a lot about cancer. I am realistic as to my prospects; I know the cancer can come back,—but I can also get run over by a car or get killed in an airplane crash. There are no guarantees for a long life. But my present lifestyle—aided by the medical experience and true caring of those I chose to help me, e.g. Dr. Warner, will assure me that I have at least the maximum possible quality of life for the years left to me. I am convinced that there are many years left.

"It is people like Dr. Warner who offer people like me (and there are many like me!) a true choice and active participation in their own recovery. It is sad that some patients are forced to go to a foreign country to receive the treatment they chose. I do not want to be deprived of my choice. I sincerely hope that you will keep this in mind when making decisions concerning Dr. Glenn Warner. We need more of his kind, not less. We need more genuine concern by the doctor and his staff for the total welfare of the human being in their care and respect for the patient's choices. I trust that you will let your concern for maintaining freedom of choice win the day." C.J.

*   *   *   *

"*Subject*: Possible hearing before your Board on Glenn Warner, M.D. regarding his qualifications to continue his Medical License and his life-work in oncology.

"I am a retired M.D. and was in General Practice in Snoqualmie, Washington from 1949 until 1986. The last 12 years of my work was in geriatrics.

"I have known Dr. Warner since he began oncology work at the Swedish Hospital Tumor Institute Clinic in 1959 and have referred to him most of my patients with known or suspected cancer disease.

"His management of these patients, and there have been many, perhaps over one hundred, has been outstanding. He was thorough and responsible in all phases of their care; diagnosis, referral to other professionals, sensible treatment, good communication with families and myself, the family doctor. Therapy-wise there were many cures, comfort and patience for all, and caring, terminal care for those incurable cancer patients we all know so well.

"But one thing stood out about Dr. Warner. The patients and families always liked him, trusted him and spoke well of him, no matter what the outcome.

"Dr. Warner has examined and treated me twice, and thankfully, for benign problems.

"Finally, it seems alarming to me that this good physician's lifework and license to continue is being threatened by other physicians who have a different view of what is good cancer treatment. If oncology was an exact science with clear and proven therapy and outcome, there might be a grain of merit in this kind of persecution but most about cancer is yet to be learned.

"The Medical Disciplinary Board would do well to recall the persecution of Dr. Ignaz Semmelweiss by the other local physicians. It was Dr. Semmelweiss who discovered that childbirth fever (post-partum infection) was being spread by the attending doctors who were not cleaning their hands, clothes and instruments. Twelve out of every hundred new mothers delivered by doctors died of this child-bed fever. He was ridiculed and forced out of Vienna by the other doctors. In the same year Lister proved that antiseptic surgery prevented infections and the world admitted that Semmelweiss was right. But it was too late—he was disgraced by his own profession and died soon after.

"Personally, Dr. Warner seems to have been a stable, sober, energetic, exemplary and productive member of our medical and social community.

"If at all possible, the Board should dismiss this matter and get on with the next case." J. W., M.D.

*   *   *   *

"I am writing this letter in support of Dr. Glenn Warner who has been my oncologist for the last 12 years—a long time for someone diagnosed as having stage III melanoma. I am deeply concerned that a group of 'well-intentioned medical professionals' may be denying patients like myself the opportunity to make a choice in their cancer treatment.

"For five and a half years I worked as a critical care nurse at the University of Washington. During that time, I cared for a number of patients acutely ill from the ravaging effects of chemotherapy and radiation therapy. Many of these patients were cured of their cancer but died of complications as a result of the treatment.

"When it was discovered that I had a distant metastasis of a recurring melanoma, I was given the option of chemotherapy and radiation with the promise that, at best, it might add an additional 3-6 months to my life. Knowing how devastating this therapy can be to the overall health of the patient, I elected to receive no therapy at all until my internist, Dr. Abby Franklin, encouraged me to consider immunotherapy offered by Dr. Glenn Warner.

"In my opinion, Dr. Warner upholds the highest standards in caring for his patients. His approach is to maximize the patient's overall physical and mental health while strengthening the patient's immunological system. The acute illness caused by chemotherapy and radiation therapy render the patient vulnerable to serious complications and great mental anguish and despair which ultimately can affect the outcome as to whether the patient lives or dies, regardless of the therapy. Dr. Warner's approach is to keep the patient as healthy as possible while fighting the cancer, an approach I feel offers the greatest hope for a full recovery.

"My experience with Dr. Warner is that he uses whatever therapy is known to work based on the most current research. With me, he used a combination of immunotherapy and chemotherapy. Never, during the three years of my treatment, did I lose a day to illness. I was able to continue working, and enjoy a very productive and active life. Eight years after completing my therapy, I became pregnant with my first child. Now I have two beautiful and robust sons.

"I truly believe that I am alive today thanks to Dr. Warner's pioneering efforts, personal dedication and undying courage in the face of the adversity posed by his colleagues. To take away Dr. Warner's medical license and thus deny patients like myself the freedom of choice, you may be condemning a multitude of patients to unnecessary and possibly death." S. D., B. S., R. N.

*   *   *   *

"It has to come to my attention that some action is in progress to withdraw Dr. Glenn Warner's license to practice medicine in this state. I cannot imagine what grievance may have been brought before your Board, but I can assure you that he is one of the most honest, forthright, and knowledgeable physicians and able practitioners that I have ever met. He is also a first class scientist who manages to keep up with the rapidly changing technological advances in the fields related to human health and medicine. I consider myself very fortunate to have been a patient of his for 25 years.

"Dr. Warner and I understand each other. I am an expert in the field of fish diseases, immunology, and nutrition. I am a consultant to an expansive international aquaculture community, research biologist, university instructor, and a pioneer in the research and development of fish biologics. Some of the fish vaccines that I developed are in use in both hemispheres, and I was responsible for the beginnings of what is now the largest manufacturer of USDA license aquatic biologics in the Americas (I am still their prime consultant), BIOMED, Inc. of Bellevue. I mention these things so that you will know that my attachment to Dr. Warner is not one of pure emotionalism. Over the years, we have followed a path of diagnostics, therapy, and prognosis based on shared discussions and not on blind faith.

"I was first diagnosed as having Hodgkin's Disease when I was 32 (I am now 57), from a pathologist's report of an excised surface lesion of the leg. I went to the Tumor Institute and began what would become a lengthy case file with Drs. Wildermuth and Warner. Specimens were sent to a number of pathologists in other cities, and confirmations were mixed (not 100% agreement). I went through a number of treatments of focused x-radiation therapy for other surface lesions over some period of time. When Dr. Warner formed his own clinic, I went with him. Dr. Warner kept a close eye on me. I never went through the other stages, but kept developing pseudo-lymphomas on a sporadic basis. We both felt strongly about immunotherapy. I was conducting my own research on the T and B cell production in fish, and have followed that path along with surgical excisions for a long time. I have discussed what we have been doing with our family physician, and a number of others in the advanced fields of immunotherapy, and all have agreed that we are fortunate to have a physician of his caliber in our region. I know that Dr. Warner discusses my case with other physicians working in the forefront of cancer therapy, as he has introduced me to them, called them while we were discussing therapeutic steps, etc. Our rapport has been genuine over the years. I frequently wonder what kind of selection process I would have to go through (if he retired) to find another oncologist as good as Warner. Right now I have another lesion that has cropped up next to an old excision, and I will plan on seeing Warner and agree to a therapeutic move. Being able to have this kind of rapport is very important to me. I sincerely hope that you will drop any actions against Dr. Warner that you might be considering." A. J. N.

*   *   *   *

"In December 1981 after finding a lump in my breast, I was referred by my doctor (not an oncologist) to a surgeon. There was never any discussion on the part of either physician as to what treatment options I had in case of malignancy. The lump proved to be malignant and when I woke up my right breast was gone. I was told that three nodes were affected. I was given an appointment with the clinic's oncologist.

"Before I saw the oncologist, I read everything I could on chemotherapy and decided that I would not allow my body to be poisoned. I met with the oncologist and the only quote I can remember from the visit was, 'I have never had a patient who could not tolerate the treatment.' Again, no other treatment was mentioned. I was not asked how I felt about the treatment, the disease, etc. It was obvious from the doctor's demeanor that I was expected to accede to everything he suggested.

"Since I had decided that I would not have chemotherapy and was not informed about alternative treatments, I was literally left with no options. Fortunately, a co-worker told me about Dr. Warner because her mother was his patient.

"I went to Dr. Warner in 1982 and he discussed immunotherapy and why he prescribed vitamins and why he expected me to engage in regular exercise. He gave me a diet which excluded caffeine, sugar, dairy products, white flour and red meats. Not unlike the Pritikin diet.

"I continue to see Dr. Warner twice a year. At the time that I had the mastectomy, I was still working. I retired from work—a profession that I had worked in for thirty years. After which I went back to school (University of Washington) and prepared myself for another career. I am now 65 and have retired again. I'm just too busy to work.

"I attribute my present state of health to the treatment which Dr. Warner prescribed and his interest and ability to involve the patient actively in his own health expectations. If Dr. Warner is in any way impeded in continuing his medical practice or harassed by the medical community, it will mean many people will have to search for a doctor or doctors who believe in the same philosophy of treatment as Dr. Warner does. It will mean many people will be disillusioned once more by an arrogant medical community which cannot countenance anything that does not follow their prescribed traditional methods." M. L. S.

*   *   *   *

"I am currently a patient of Dr. Glenn Warner and have been since February 2, 1967. My original cancer, adeno carcinoma of the cervix, was discovered by Dr. John Barnes of Richland, Washington and he referred me to the Swedish Tumor Clinic. This was my first contact with Dr. Glenn Warner.

"I was treated successfully with two sessions of radium insertions. I stayed with the Tumor Clinic until Dr. Glenn Warner established his own practice and at that time I had any follow-ups necessary with Dr. Warner.

"My quality of life after the initial recovery period has been very good and I have received very excellent and loving care from Dr. Warner. In March 20, 1981, a doctor saw a melanoma on my leg, which turned out to be a nodular type level 4, and referred me to a Seattle surgeon. At that time, I called Dr. Warner and he saw me and referred me to Dr. Clark Hoffman on March 25, 1981 who performed surgery on me and then followed my recovery along with Dr. Warner. Again, my recovery and quality of life have been very good.

"I feel that for the past 22 years Dr. Warner has been giving me the very best of medical care and his concern for my personal well being. He has also helped me to lead a healthy daily life during these past years." C. L. H.

*   *   *   *

"This is a hard letter to write, it stirs up so many emotions. When someone helps to save the life of someone you love dearly, it is an emotional topic—very emotional. However, there are also facts in this letter that bear your serious attention. I implore you to listen to both the medical facts and to my truth-filled emotion. First, I must express my disgust that this issue has come before the Board at all. How despicable! And it says more about the integrity and character of those bringing the 'charges' then it will ever say about Dr. Warner. I will also say that I am not surprised, given the oppression that often happens to true leaders and pioneers. But beyond my disgust and probably more important—is my real sadness and grief that a man such as Dr. Warner should have to deal with this at all. It makes me truly sad.

"Moving on to other things....I am a health care professional myself, with 20 years of varied experience working as an R.N. However, I am writing to you primarily as a daughter here.

"When my Dad got a serious cancer, I began to research all of the literature for information to be a resource and source of hope for him. I'll be brief about my Dad's saga: he had his first surgery for cancer of the stomach 10 years ago and the second one 6 years ago. Dr. Warner entered our lives 6 years ago after Dad had had his entire stomach removed and cancer found extensively in his lymph nodes. He had been treated by another oncology physician (Randy Trowbridge, Everett, Washington) up until this time and had had opinions of 2 other physicians (Peter Wasserman, Seattle and another oncology doctor in Everett). My Dad himself selected Dr. Warner as his doctor. He was impressed with his experience, knowledge and the holistic program offered. And, although he didn't mention it, I would guess also by his caring, committed manner. I had remembered Dr. Warner from when I was a student at Seattle University and was working one summer for expenses, as a receptionist at Swedish Hospital Tumor Institute (about 1968). Dr. Warner was on the staff there then....I remembered him still for his truly caring manner. He was the Dr. who was there after everyone else had gone home, spending time with patients and families, reviewing records, etc. And he always spent more time than everyone else on regular appointments. He impressed me as a human being at that time in an unforgettable way. Then later (about 15 years), when my Dad was in the hospital with his second cancer surgery, I happened to see Dr. Warner on TV being interviewed about the immune system and cancer. Given all my recent research, I was impressed all over again. Knowing that my Dad was searching for a new Dr., and thinking it might be a good match, I suggested he get an opinion from Dr. Warner. And, as I have mentioned, he selected Dr. Warner. For a man facing a life or death situation (with most traditional oncologists writing his situation off as death only), to find someone to help him with this struggle that he had confidence in was key.

"As you know, cancer of the stomach with extensive lymph node involvement is an almost unwinnable situation by traditional medical/oncology standards. The grim statistics we were given by the other oncologists confirm this. Well, it is 6 years later and my Dad continues living the life he wants to live. I will not mislead you that it has been easy in any sense—emotionally or physically. But I will tell you he has felt well most all of the time and that he leads the life he wants—and at 70 years could outwork most of us. He had extensive tests this past summer related to a different problem as it turned out (now remedied) and no trace of cancer was found in his body, as has been the case for several years now. Dr. Warner's holistic program and immunotherapy have absolutely been key in his recovery. And I am convinced (and the statistics confirm this) had he followed the traditional approach that was suggested by other doctors, he would have died about five years ago.

"As you must know, the work that Dr. Warner has been involved with involving immunology is now becoming accepted as a key to disease in general. Also, the wisest health practitioners use a holistic approach to wellness and disease.

"Dr. Warner deserves nothing but your respect and admiration. If a loved one of yours should develop a serious cancer, they would be most blessed to have him as their doctor. We are fortunate indeed that he lives and practices in the Northwest…for his knowledge and skill as a clinician and for his integrity as a human being. (My mother said recently that Dr. Warner is the Dr. Savauge of cancer care).

"In conclusion, (I've tried to be brief unsuccessfully and there's much I haven't said), my Dad still believes that doctors are basically smart people though he has come to know that they don't always agree on important things. I implore you to see past personal threat, pettiness and whatever else may be involved here and get to the truth (if a hearing is required at all). If you must make a decision, make one that reflects the best interests of patients and serves us all well. And you, yes you, on the Medical Disciplinary Board, don't let my Dad down about doctors." J. S.

*   *   *   *

"I have been a patient of Dr. Warner for three years. My ovarian cancer was diagnosed during a hysterectomy in October 1985 in Everett, Washington. Subsequently, the Everett doctors recommended chemotherapy. After the chemotherapy treatment ended in August 1986, the Everett doctors said nothing about rehabilitation of my body. My white count was very low and my immune system was not functioning normally. The only thing the Everett doctors suggested was a second surgery just to see if they had done everything right!

"In August 1986, I conferred with Dr. Warner about my condition and the need for a second surgery. He assured me, that with his treatment, my immune system could return to normal more quickly and through blood tests and tumor markers, he could monitor any recurrences of cancer.

"With Dr.Warner's positive treatment of nutrition and exercise and blood tests, my immune system is normal. I eat more healthful foods and avoid foods that could aggravate tumors and I am on a regular exercise program.

"My quality of life has been wonderful since I have been under Dr. Warner's treatment. And I didn't have to have the second surgery which proved to be unnecessary.

"I support Dr. Warner 100% and his treatment. I am one of the hundreds of people that are going to be very upset if you restrict, in any way, the practice of this intelligent, caring and hardworking physician." B. L.

*   *   *   *

"We were very concerned to recently learn that Dr. Glenn Warner is facing some sort of disciplinary problem.

"In 1967 my wife was diagnosed with a particularly dangerous type of melanoma. In Port Angeles, Washington, our home at the time, her doctor advised me that the prognosis was exceedingly grim. After a long period of treatments, she was also advised by cancer specialists at the Mayo Clinic that the situation was quite hopeless and that she should return home and put her affairs in order. This was done.

"But, soon after leaving Rochester, she was referred to Dr. Warner, probably in early 1968. From the first, he was optimistic, encouraging, steadfast. A long series of traditional and non-traditional treatments followed. At first she continued to have major problems including the loss of a kidney to a tumor. Her body weight fell rapidly She became very weak.

"Through all this—a period of months that became years—Dr. Warner was always cheerful, supportive, hopeful and optimistic. Always he had the time, at bleak and late hours, for concerned family members. His skill and devotion and 'never give up' attitude has sustained her for 21 years.

"And what is the result of all this? Today, at age 63, she is trim, athletic, doing hours of aerobics each week with frequent beach and mountain hikes. Her health and appearance are excellent.

"I'm sure that neither of us have ever met a more competent and devoted physician. We urge you to consider the skill and dedication of this kindly healer who has done so much for our family." K. D. B.

*   *   *   *

"I am deeply hurt to think anyone in the medical profession could go so far to unjustly criticize or try to take Dr. Warner's medical license away from him. I owe my life to this professional and caring man. I would not be alive today had he not given me his medical and psychological understanding and care.

"I have been under Dr. Warner's care since 1978 for breast carcinoma. Within eight months I had two more major surgeries, and I am deeply thankful to Dr. Warner for helping me through a most difficult time in my life.

"Dr. Warner's medical treatment gave me a reason to live and a quality of life that has helped me overcome many problems.

"I have a history of family cancer. My two sisters have died as a result of breast cancer, radiation and chemotherapy. My brother also died as a result of cancer. My family feels that I am a 'medical wonder' since I have never had chemotherapy or radiation treatments. Dr. Warner's program taught me to live and control the everyday stress of working for Vashon School District. I was able to return to work as librarian very soon after surgeries.

"How can you destroy this man? He has given the best quality care available in the medical profession to all his patients.

"I am ever grateful to Dr. Warner for my health today. I owe him my life, which is more than I can say for my two sisters and brother. They were not as fortunate as myself for they died not having the experience of his excellent medical treatment. If they had been under his care, perhaps all three would be alive today.

"I am very upset. I feel the Medical Disciplinary Board has made a terrible and unjust accusation against Dr. Warner." D. R. N.

*   *   *   *

"I am writing in support of Dr. Glenn Warner. I was diagnosed with Osteogenic Sarcoma in March 1983 at the age of 21. My left leg was amputated by Dr. Ernest Burgess and subsequently I was referred by Dr. Burgess to Dr. Warner for follow-up care.

"I have lived all over the country since 1983 and, due to a recurrence of cancer in my lungs in July 1986, have had the 'opportunity' to sample the expertise of many doctors. I have been under the care of physicians at Memorial Sloan-Kettering, Massachusetts General, and the Mayo Clinic, among others. Although all were fine doctors in the technical sense, their cumulative bedside manner rivaled that of a sty-rofoam cup.

"Throughout these years Dr. Warner has stood as a shining beacon of hope amongst a sea of doomsayers. He has never suggested that I forgo traditional treatment when it was warranted. He has suggested adjuvant therapies such as diet and mental imagery to complement traditional treatments. He has urged me to take control of my illness rather than leaving all decisions to the doctors. He has urged me to pursue a physical conditioning program akin to that of an Olympic athlete and, today, I am a member of the U.S. Disabled Ski Team and a candidate for the 1992 Olympic games. These therapies may not be sanctioned by the traditional medical community as effective but the fact that I am cancer-free more than three years after my recurrence is good enough for me.

"The night after my amputation, Dr. Warner sat on the edge of my bed and told me that I could look at the situation three ways: 1) I could see it as the end of the world, 2) I could pretend that nothing had happened and go on with life as before, or 3) I could look at the experience as a chance to grow and to better my life. I will never forget those words.

"It is a pity that the bulk of medical professionals no longer understand what the word 'care' means. Those that would deny Dr. Warner the right to care for his patients are doing us, as well as the entire community, a grave injustice." J. C. C.

*   *   *   *

"I am writing in regards to the upcoming hearing for Dr. Glenn Warner. I have been a patient of his ever since I was diagnosed as having a fibrosarcoma in the summer of 1973. I was 14 years old at the time.

"After my diagnosis and referral by Dr. Ralph Rinne of Bellingham, Washington, I saw Dr. Warner bi-weekly for several years. After my initial surgery to remove the tumor in 1973, a second surgery was required a year later, as was a lower left lobectomy in the fall of 1975 due to metastases.

"The primary method of treatment used by Dr. Warner in my case was 'BCG' therapy to stimulate the immune system. I noticed a rather dramatic change in my ability to fight off disease and illness with the immunotherapy. Prior to treatments, I was often sick with colds, flu, etc., seeming to 'catch anything that was going around'. Since undergoing therapy, I have been very resistant to illness—often coming out without so much as a sniffle, while most everyone around me is sick.

"I have appreciated the fact that Dr. Warner was not quick to bring out the 'heavy artillery', so-to-speak, of cancer treatment even considering the severity of my disease. Not that he was negligent in any way either. I always felt he was monitoring very carefully my condition. His recommendations were always very sensible and practical, such as having his patients follow a health-conscious diet, avoid any undue stress, get proper rest, exercise, etc.

"I have been free of any disease now for 14 years. I lead a very active life as the proud and grateful mother of four healthy sons. Most people are amazed at the things I accomplish notwithstanding my past history of disease. From my understanding, it is a miracle that I even survived past my high school years, let alone lived to experience almost 13 years of marriage as well as four very easy pregnancies and deliveries. In looking back, I have given many thanks that Dr. Warner avoided such treatments as radiation and chemotherapy. Even while undergoing my 'treatments'. I was able to carry on a normal life, unaffected by the usual side-effects of more traditional methods of treatment (nausea, hair-loss, weakness, etc.).

"I consider my self completely healed of disease. I am grateful that God allowed Dr. Warner to have a part in this miracle. I hope this testimony will have a positive affect on your decision." C. A. K.

*   *   *   *

"I am writing in regard to Dr. Warner: I have been a patient of his for two years. When I was first diagnosed with cancer, I was told by my doctor in Tacoma, Washington (Robert Theissen) there was no one here who could treat my type of cancer. He sent me to the University of Washington, (Dr. David Figge). I have Endometrial Stromal Sarcoma. Dr. Figge, at the University, did a simple pelvic exam and scheduled surgery. He was going to do a colostomy and an ileostomy, an 11 hour operation. I asked Dr. Figge if I had any alternatives. He said, 'Without the operation, you will die.' I went in for surgery. It was not successful. After leaving me open for 4 hours, they closed me up. The consensus was, they could do the radical operation, but I would still have cancer. After 12 days in the hospital, I was told there was nothing they could do for me. I went back to Dr. Theissen who wanted to do chemotherapy even though my type of cancer doesn't respond to chemo! (His words). Before I would agree to do this, I wanted to see what Dr. Warner had to say. My first visit was very encouraging. He wanted me to eat better, get plenty of exercise, listen to good music, etc. (Improve my quality of life). Dr. Warner has a positive attitude and passes that on to his patients.

"When I first saw Dr. Warner, the cancer was in both of my lungs and all through the pelvic area. After two years of treatment, (Interferon, Immune therapy, hormone manipulation, and some radiation), I am happy to say my cancer has diminished to one small tumor in the lower pelvic area. (WITHOUT SIDE EFFECTS).

"I am living a full life. I work full time and have time with my family. I owe this to Dr. Warner." J. C. R.

*   *   *   *

"In May 1985, I had a swollen lymph node removed from my neck. The pathology was hysticocytic lymphoma. I was sent to a 'conventional' oncologist. When he got through talking to me, I felt hopeless, helpless, and totally terrorized. He gave me doomsday statistics (85% chance of this recurring in two years, then fatal in short period of time, etc.). Even though I had already had all the tests and no other cancer was found in my body, he still wanted to radiate. I told him I wanted a more holistic approach to my healing and he told me he didn't support that concept.

"I then told everyone I knew what was going on with me and how I wanted to handle my recovery and asked if anyone knew of any doctor who would help me. That's how I found Glenn Warner. I told him what kind of care I was looking for and he gave it to me. He also gave me hope, he empowered me, he showed me how I could be in charge of my wellness to an extent I never thought possible. He did not find it necessary to radiate something that wasn't there. He sees me every three months for extensive blood work and a thorough examination. I have been cancer-free since the tumor was removed. Today I am healthier than I have ever been, I look better than I ever have, and I am grateful to this man for showing me how to live.

"No one is forced to go to any one doctor. Dr. Warner is not treating anyone against his/her will. He is offering a choice, an alternative that many people want today. I am appalled that your actions may take away my freedom of choice for my own health care. I want body/mind/emotion/spirit healing; treating only the body is not enough anymore. Dr. Warner has maintained a practice for as long as he has because people have wanted his kind of care. We want it to continue" M. T.

*   *   *   *

"I have been a patient of Dr. Glenn Warner since February 1976. He was recommended to me by Dr. Charles MacMahon, at that time a well known and respected physician and surgeon at Swedish Hospital. I had a lymphomic tumor in the orbit of my left eye.

"At this time, Dr. John Hicks surgically removed as much of the tumor as possible. For fear of me losing my eyesight, they could not remove it all. At this time the subject of radiation came up. My wife and I talked with a radiologist at the Swedish Hospital Tumor

Institute. We did not feel comfortable with his recommendation. We talked it out with Dr. Warner and because of the location of the tumors and the amount of radiation needed at that time, we chose to go with chemotherapy. The tumors were kept under control with Dr. Warner's care until 1987. The tumor in the right eye was completely gone but the one in the left eye started to grow.

"With eleven years of excellent care and much more knowledge of my body and cancer under Dr. Warner, it was time for the big step. I again had surgery (Dr. John Hicks) which Dr. Warner followed with radiation. Yes, I was scared but comfortable with the decision. Two years have gone by and there is no indication that a tumor exists in either of my eyes. I will continue to be under Dr. Warner's care as long as necessary.

"In the fall of 1975 I was diagnosed by an optomologist as having a stopped up tear duct in my eye. When it failed to go away, I decided to seek another opinion. I often wonder what my future would have been without Dr. Hicks and Dr. Warner.

"I am at a loss to even try to comprehend why any person let alone someone in the medical profession would attack Dr. Warner's credibility or principles. He has not only been my doctor over the past twelve years, he has become my trusted friend. I will be sixty-two years of age next month. I strongly feel Dr. Warner has played a significant role in the quality of those years and, hopefully, for years to come." J. A. R.

PART IV

HISTORY OF CANCER RESEARCH AND TREATMENT

CHAPTER 19

THE IMMUNE SYSTEM & IMMUNOTHERAPY

Scientists have been trying to unlock the mystery of the immune system for over 100 years. With the discoveries made in research as discussed in Chapter 22, it would seem that it should be fully understood by now. When our immune system is not functioning properly, our doctor should be able to fix it, but it is a wondrous and complex mechanism.

So what exactly is known about our immune system? It has long been known that it is a network of cells and organs that work together to defend the body against attacks by foreign invaders. These are primarily germs—tiny infection-causing organisms such as bacteria and viruses, as well as parasites and fungi. Because the human body provides an ideal environment for many germs, or microbes, it is constantly attacked. It is the job of the immune system to keep these foreign invaders out or, failing that, to seek them out and destroy them. When the immune system misfires, however, or when it is crippled, it can unleash a torrent of diseases—allergy or arthritis or cancer or AIDS.

The immune system is amazingly complex. It can recognize millions of different enemies, and it can produce secretions and cells to match up with and wipe out each one of them. The secret to its success is an elaborate and dynamic communications network: millions and millions of cells, organized into sets and subsets, pass information back and forth like clouds of bees swarming around a hive. Once immune cells receive the alarm, they undergo strategic changes and begin to produce powerful chemicals. These substances allow the cells to regulate their own growth and behavior, enlist their fellows, and direct new recruits to trouble spots. At the heart of the immune system is a remarkable ability to distinguish between the body's own cells (self) and foreign cells (nonself). The body's immune defenses normally coexist peacefully with cells that carry distinctive "self" marker molecules. But when immune defenders encounter cells or organisms carrying markers that say "foreign" they quickly swing into action.

Anything that can trigger this immune response is called an *antigen*. An antigen can be a germ such as a virus, or even part of a virus. Tissues or cells from another person (except an identical twin) also carry nonself markers and act as antigens; this explains why tissue transplants are rejected. In abnormal situations, the immune system can mistake self for nonself and attack it; the result is called an autoimmune disease. Some forms of arthritis and diabetes are autoimmune diseases. In other cases, the immune system responds inappropriately to a seemingly harmless substance such as ragweed pollen or cat hair; the result is allergy, and this kind of antigen is called an *allergen*.

*　　　*　　　*　　　*

Through years of study and discoveries by many different research scientists, the structure of the immune system is pretty much understood. What seems to elude the scientific world is how to duplicate the efforts of our body's immune responses to repair such deficiencies as occur in cancer. The organs of the immune system are positioned throughout the body. They are called *lymphoid organs* because they are home to *lymphocytes*, small white blood cells that are the key players in the immune system. These lymphocytes are made in the *bone marrow*, the soft tissue in the hollow center of bones. Bone marrow is the ultimate source of all blood cells, including white blood cells destined to become immune cells. Lymphocytes known as T-cells mature in the *thymus*, an organ that lies behind the breastbone.

Lymphocytes can travel throughout the body, using either the *blood vessels* or their own system of *lymphatic vessels*. Like small creeks that empty into larger and larger rivers, the lymphatic vessels feed into larger and larger channels. At the base of the neck they merge into a large duct, which discharges its contents into the bloodstream. The lymphatic vessels carry *lymph*, a clear fluid that bathes the body's tissues.

Small, bean-shaped *lymph nodes* are laced along the lymphatic vessels, with clusters in the neck, armpits, abdomen, and groin. Each lymph node contains specialized compartments where immune cells congregate, and where they can encounter antigens.

The *spleen* is a fist-sized organ at the upper left of the abdomen. Like the lymph nodes, the spleen contains specialized compartments where immune cells gather and work, and serves as a meeting ground where antigens confront the immune defenses.

Clumps of lymphoid tissue are found in many parts of the body, especially in the linings of the digestive tract and the airways and lungs—territories that serve as gateways to the body. These tissues include the *tonsils*, the *adenoids,* and the *appendix.*

*   *   *   *

Immune cells and foreign particles enter the lymph nodes via incoming lymphatic vessels or the lymph nodes' tiny blood vessels. All lymphocytes exit lymph nodes through outgoing lymphatic vessels. Once in the bloodstream, they are transported to tissues throughout the body. They patrol everywhere for foreign antigens, then gradually drift back into the lymphatic system, to begin the cycle all over again.

The immune system stockpiles a huge arsenal of cells, not only lymphocytes but also cell-devouring phagocytes and their relatives. Some immune cells take on all comers, while others are trained on highly specific targets. To work effectively, most immune cells need the cooperation of their fellows. Sometimes immune cells communicate by direct physical contact, sometimes by releasing chemical messengers.

In order to have room for all the cells needed to match millions of possible enemies, the immune system stores just a few of each kind. When an antigen appears, those few matching cells multiply into a full-scale army. After their job is done, they fade away.

Lymphocytes are one of the main types of immune cells. And B and T cells are the main types of lymphocytes. *B cells* work chiefly by secreting soluble substances called *antibodies* into the body's fluids. Antibodies ambush antigens circulating in the bloodstream; however, they are powerless to penetrate cells. The job of attacking target cells—either cells that have been infected by viruses or cells that have been distorted by cancer—is left to T lymphocytes or other immune cells.

Each B cell is programmed to make one specific antibody. For example, one B cell will make an antibody that blocks a virus that causes the common cold, while another produces an antibody that attacks a bacterium that causes pneumonia.

When a B cell encounters its triggering antigen, it gives rise to many large cells known as *plasma cells*. Every plasma cell is essentially a factory for producing antibody. Each of the plasma cells descended from a given B cell manufactures millions of identical antibody molecules and pours them into the bloodstream.

An antibody matches an antigen much as a key matches a lock. Some match exactly, others fit more like a skeleton key. But whenever antibody and antigen interlock, the antibody marks the antigen for destruction.

Antibodies belong to a family of large molecules known as *immunoglobulins*. Different types play different roles in the immune defense strategy. Immunoglobulin G, or IgG, works efficiently to coat microbes, speeding their uptake by other cells in the immune system. Immunoglobulin M is very effective in killing bacteria. Immunoglobulin A concentrates in body fluids—tears, saliva, the secretions of the respiratory tract and the digestive tract—guarding entrances to the body. Immunoglobulin, whose natural job probably is to protect against parasite infections, is the villain responsible for the symptoms of allergy.

T cells contribute to the immune defenses in two major ways. Some direct and regulate the immune responses. Others are killer cells that attack cells that are infected or cancerous. Less helpfully, killer T cells assail foreign cells transplanted as organ grafts.

T lymphocytes work primarily by secreting potent chemical messages known as *cytokines* or, more specifically, *lymphokines*. Binding to target cells, lymphokines mobilize many other cells and substances. They encourage the growth of cells, trigger cell activity, direct cell traffic, destroy target cells, and arouse phagocytes.

Natural killer cells (NK cells) are another kind of lethal white cell, or lymphocyte. Like killer T cells, NK cells are armed with granules filled with potent chemicals. But killer T cells attack only their specific matching targets; natural killer cells attack any foe. Both kinds of killer cells slay on contact. The deadly assassin binds to its target, aims its weapons, and then delivers a lethal burst of chemicals.

Phagocytes (or 'cell eaters') are large white cells that can swallow and digest microbes and other foreign particles. *Monocytes* are phagocytes that circulate in the blood. When monocytes migrate into tissues, they develop into *macrophages*, or 'big eaters.' Specialized types of macrophages can be found in many organs, including the lungs, the kidneys, the brain, and the liver.

Macrophages play many roles. As scavengers, they rid the body of worn-out cells and other debris. They display bits of foreign antigen in a way that draws the attention of matching lymphocytes. And they churn out an amazing variety of powerful cytokines, known as *monokines*, which are vital to the immune responses.

Granulocytes are another kind of immune cell. Granulocytes are white blood cells that contain granules filled with potent chemicals, which allow the granulocytes to destroy microorganisms. Some of these chemicals such as histamine also contribute to inflammation and allergy.

One type of granulocyte, the *neutrophil*, is also a phagocyte; it uses its prepackaged chemicals to degrade the microbes it ingests. *Eosinophils* and *basophils* are granulocytes that "degranulate", spraying their chemicals onto harmful cells or microbes nearby.

The *mast cell* is a twin of the basophil, except that it is not a blood cell. Rather, it is found in the lungs, skin, tongue, and the linings of the nose and intestinal tract, where it is responsible for the symptoms of allergy.

A related structure is a cell fragment, the blood *platelet*. Platelets, too, contain granules. In addition to promoting blood clotting and wound repair, platelets activate some of the immune defenses. The *complement system* is made up of about 25 body chemicals that work together to "complement" the action of antibodies in destroying bacteria. Complement also helps to rid the body of antibody-coated antigens (*antigen-antibody complexes*). Complement proteins, which cause blood vessels to become dilated and then leaky, contribute to the redness, warmth, swelling, pain, and loss of function that characterize an *inflammatory response*.

*   *   *   *

Complement proteins circulate in the blood in an inactive form. When the first protein in the complement series is activated—typically by antibody that has locked onto an antigen protruding from a cell—it sets in motion a domino effect. Each component takes its turn in a precise chain in steps known as the 'complement cascade.' The end product is a cylinder entered into—and puncturing a hole in—the cell's wall. With fluids and molecules flowing in and out, the cell swells and bursts.

How does our body mount an immune response? Microbes attempting to get into the body must first move past the body's external armor. The skin and the membranes lining the body's gateways not only pose a physical barrier, they are also rich in scavenger cells and IgA antibodies.

Next, invaders must escape a series of *nonspecific* defenses, which are ready to attack, without regard for any specific antigen markers. These include patrolling scavenger cells, natural killer (NK) cells, and complement.

Microbes that cross the nonspecific barriers must then confront *specific* weapons tailored just for them. Specific weapons, which include both antibodies and cells, are equipped with singular receptor structures that allow them to recognize and interact with their designated targets.

Long ago, physicians realized that people who had recovered from the plague would never get it again. They had acquired immunity. This is because, whenever T cells and B cells are activated, some of the cells become *memory cells*. The next time that an individual meets up with the same antigen, the immune system is set to demolish it.

Immunity can be strong or weak, short-lived or long-lasting, depending on the type of antigen, the amount of antigen, and the route by which it enters the body. Immunity can also be influenced by the genes you inherit; when faced with the same antigen, some individuals will respond forcefully, others, feebly, and some, not at all.

An immune response can be sparked not only by infection but also by immunization with vaccines. *Vaccines* contain microorganisms—or parts of microorganisms—which have been treated so they will be able to provoke an immune response but not full-blown disease.

Immunity can also be transferred from one individual to another by injections of serum rich in antibodies (*antiserum*). Immune serum globulin or 'gamma globulin' is sometimes given to protect travelers to countries where hepatitis is widespread, but such 'passive immunity' typically lasts only a few weeks or months.

The cells of the immune system, like other cells, can grow uncontrollably; the result is cancer. *Leukemias* are caused by the proliferation of white blood cells, or leukocytes. The uncontrolled growth of antibody-producing plasma cells can lead to *multiple myeloma*. Cancers of the lymphoid organs, known as *lymphomas*, include Hodgkin's disease.

*   *   *   *

The immune system provides one of the body's main defenses against cancer. When normal cells turn into cancer cells, some of the antigens on their surface may change. These new or altered antigens can flag immune defenders, including killer T cells, natural killer cells, and macrophages. According to one theory, patrolling cells of the immune system provide body wide surveillance, spying out and eliminating cells that become cancerous. Tumors develop when the system breaks down or is overwhelmed.

Scientists are shaping immune cells and substances into ingenious new anticancer weapons. Substances known as *biological response modifiers*, including lymphocytes and lymphokines, are being used to bolster the patient's immune response. In some cases, biological response modifiers are injected directly into the patient; in other cases they are used in the laboratory to transform some of the patient's own lymphocytes into tumor-hungry cells which are then injected back into the patient, so they can attack the cancer cells.

Antibodies specially made to recognize specific cancers could be coupled with drugs, toxins, or radioactive materials, then sent off like 'magic bullets' to deliver their lethal cargo directly to the target cancer cells. Alternatively, toxins can be linked to a lymphokine and routed to cells equipped with receptors for the lymphokine. Radioactively labeled antibodies can also be used to track down hidden nests of cancers, (metastases).

Evidence is mounting that the immune system and the nervous system are linked in several ways. One well-known connection involves the adrenal glands. In response to stress messages from the brain, the adrenal glands release hormones into the blood. In addition to helping a person respond to emergencies by mobilizing the body's energy reserves, these 'stress hormones' can stifle the effects of antibodies and lymphocytes. Hormones and other chemicals known to convey messages among nerve cells have been found to 'speak' to cells of the immune system. Indeed, some immune cells are able to manufacture typical nerve cells products, while some lymphokines can transmit information to the nervous system. What's more, the brain may send messages to the immune system directly, down nerve cells; networks of nerve fibers have been found connecting to the lymphoid organs.

Scientists are now able to mass-produce immune cell secretions, both antibodies and lymphokines, as well as specialized immune cells. The ready supply of these materials not only has revolutionized the study of the immune system itself, but also has had an enormous impact on medicine, agriculture, and industry.

So-called *monoclonal antibodies* are identical antibodies made by the many descendants (clones) of a single plasma cell. Typically, the target antigen is injected into a mouse, then antibody-producing plasma cells are 'harvested' from the mouse. The mouse plasma cell is fused with a long-lived laboratory-grown plasma cell, within a single cell membrane. These fused cells, or hybrids, are then cloned. A clone will secrete, over a long period of time, the made-to-order monoclonal (clone) antibody.

Genetic engineering allows scientists to pluck genes—segments of the hereditary material, DNA—from one type of organism and combine them with genes of a second organism. In this way, relatively simple organisms such as bacteria or yeast can be induced to make quantities of human proteins, including hormones such as insulin as well as lymphokines and monokines. They can also manufacture proteins from infectious agents such as the hepatitis virus or the AIDS virus, for use in vaccines. Genetic engineering also opens the door for *gene therapy*; replacing defective or missing genes or adding helpful genes.

With this wealth of knowledge, acquired over many years, where are we in relation to cancer treatments? Is the individual patient benefiting from all this information? Since mainstream medicine is still adamant that surgery, radiation and/or chemotherapy are the only acceptable options for the cancer patient, the answer seems to be no.

It is all the more amazing to me that a doctor such as Glenn Warner has been using biologic response modifiers (such as BCG and other immune stimulants) since the early 1970s. It took a great deal of courage to go this route in an attempt to save his patients' lives and give them a good quality of life while undergoing treatment. I was one of the beneficiaries of this approach.

CHAPTER 20

THE MIND/BODY CONNECTION

Warner is not alone in believing that the mind/body connection contributes to the wellness of patients. There are dozens of books available to support the belief that there is more to treating cancer then simply attacking the tumor. The authors of these books are respectable, intelligent, knowledgeable professional practitioners who have come to pretty much the same conclusion and that is the absolute necessity of treating the whole person with a variety of methods. The problem seems to be that it requires more from most doctors then they are willing to give.

O. Carl Simonton, M.D. was one of the first to recognize the benefits of a physical/mental/spiritual approach to cancer. Since 1971, he has treated thousands of patients and has documented studies that prove that involving the patient contributes to the success of the treatment program.

Simonton began his medical residency confident that he could contribute to a cure for cancer. However, he says, "I had not considered that a patient might have something to do with whether or not a treatment worked. I was amazed that many of my patients didn't seem motivated to get better. They not only had no confidence in their own ability to get well, they had no confidence in me or any other doctor treating them for cancer."

This set Simonton on a search to find ways to mobilize his patients' inner resources and in 1978 he co-authored a book, *Getting Well Again*. In 1992, he published *The Healing Journey, Restoring Health and Harmony to Body, Mind and Spirit* with Reid Henson and Brenda Hampton. Simonton believes, and has proven through randomized studies, that patients do better when attention is paid to them as human beings.

In his book, *The Healing Journey*, Simonton tells of studies conducted by others that substantiate what he found with his own patients. He mentions a controlled, randomized study by Dr. David Spiegel of Stanford University which showed that the patient with support lived twice as long as the patient with no counseling. Other studies by the New York Academy of Sciences, C.B. Thomas of Johns Hopkins Medical School, and Stephen Greer at Kings College Hospital in London reinforced the amazing success of Simonton's patients.

During the past ten years, the emphasis of Simonton's work has been to find how the mind can be used to influence the body most effectively. He says, "I believe that the power of the mind goes far beyond what I first imagined. In addition, I believe that, beyond the body and mind, there is another aspect of healing that needs to be addressed: the spiritual aspect....Our work with patients has demonstrated that health involves body, mind and spirit. And while the mind alone can be used to influence physical state, it is used most effectively when it is aware of spirit. Spirit gives us resources that can't be reached through traditional psychological approaches. It opens us to healing forces that go far beyond our current understanding of our own limits. And we can learn to bring that power into our lives."

It is hard work to examine your life, your attitudes, your goals to make life-altering changes. The results, however, can be miraculous and lead to a life of joy.

*   *   *   *

Dr. Bernie S. Siegel, surgeon, was taught in medical school not to get involved with his patients and felt like a failure the first years of his practice. After attending a seminar led by oncologist O. Carl Simonton and psychologist Stephanie Matthew on *Psychological Factors, Stress and Cancer* in 1978, his whole approach to the practice of medicine changed. In 1986, he published *Love, Medicine and Miracles*. It's a wonderful book full of love and hope. When Siegel speaks of his patients, he is mindful of what they have taught him about healing. He calls the patients who take charge and become involved 'exceptional patients.'

Siegel says, "I personally feel that we do have 'live' and 'die' mechanisms within us. Other doctors' scientific research and my own day-to-day clinical experience have convinced me that the state of mind changes the state of the body by working through the central nervous system. Peace of mind sends the body a 'live' message, while depression, fear and unresolved conflict give it a 'die' message. Thus, all healing is scientific, even if science can't yet explain exactly how the unexpected miracles occur.

"Exceptional patients manifest the will to live in its most potent form. They take charge of their lives even if they were never able to before, and they work hard to achieve health and peace of mind. They do not rely on doctors to take the initiative but rather use them as members of a team, demanding the utmost in technique, resourcefulness, concern, and open-mindedness. If they're not satisfied, they change doctors."

In his second book, *Peace, Love and Healing*, published in 1989, Siegel expands on the subject of his first book and shares what he has learned. In his own words, he explains that the emphasis is "self-healing, that ability given to us by our Creator and too long neglected by medicine. That does not mean that I am advocating turning one's back on the medical profession——but I also do not believe in relying on it alone. Modern medicine and self-healing need not and should not be mutually exclusive. I advise using all options, which include your innate ability to heal, as well as what science has to offer."

Siegel places great emphasis on the doctor/patient relationship. He speaks of the doctor as a facilitator in the process of getting well. He points out that the doctors cannot always cure but they can always care and that it is important for the physician to continue to offer hope as long as the patient wants to continue fighting.

*   *   *   *

Many of you will be familiar with Norman Cousin's book, *Anatomy of an Illness*. Instead of accepting a death sentence for an incurable disease, he embarked on his own healing program and completely recovered. Years later, when he had a heart attack, he refused medical intervention and chose instead to completely change his lifestyle. He lived many more years and, in fact, was hired by UCLA Medical Center to work with their doctors and teach them how to relate to their patients in a more loving and humane way.

*   *   *   *

Harold H. Benjamin, Ph.D., founded the Wellness Community in Santa Monica, California in 1982. The success of this cancer center prompted him to write *From Victim to Victor*. It is a guide to the possibilities of surviving even the most dire diagnosis of cancer. It's about accepting the diagnosis but not the verdict, of marshaling all resources in this life and death battle. He explodes the myth that an individual with cancer must accept passively whatever fate has in store. He calls us to be the Patient Active, taking part in decisions and changing negative patterns in our lives. Visualization, meditation, relaxation, stress reduction, immune system enhancement as well as guidelines for the patient/physician relationship are all discussed in this book.

Every book I have read on this subject talks about going from hopelessness to hope. We are all going to die someday, but we can live the life we have with greater joy and inner peace.

*   *   *   *

Larry Dossey, M.D., former chief of staff of Hunaba Medical City, Dallas, is devoting full time to writing, lecturing and consulting on the power of prayer. He is the author of *Space, Time & Medicine, Beyond Illness, Recovering the Soul,* and *Meaning & Medicine and Healing Words: The Power of Prayer and the Practice of Medicine.*

Dossey explains his philosophy when he says that for years he thought that prayer was not in the same ballpark with drugs and surgery, so he didn't pray for his patients. He thought prayer was sort of a frill. But he continually encountered so much solid, scientific evidence that prayer works that he decided he had to make a place for prayer in his life as a physician—-for the health of his patients.

Praying for his patients gave Dossey a great feeling of satisfaction and peace. Through prayer, he felt that he extended another dimension of reality to them as well as bringing them the best that technical medicine had to offer. He applied a different dimension—a sacred dimension—of therapy to their care. He felt as if he covered not just most of the bases, but maybe all of them. What began to get his attention about prayer were cases in which people had life-threatening diseases and chose prayer in place of medical treatment—and the amazing thing was that they got well.

Dossey recounts the case of a patient with metastatic lung cancer who elected to have no medical treatment at all. Instead, he relied on prayer support from his church. A year later he came back to the hospital for an x-ray and it was completely normal.

This case was early in Dr. Dossey's medical career and it was so astonishing and unexplainable that he ignored its implications. It wasn't until years later and other 'miraculous' healings that he began to seriously examine the power of prayer. It was then that he began to discover scientific evidence that proves prayer works.

He goes on to cite the work of Dr. William Braud and others in the field of imagery and prayer. More than 130 laboratory studies have been done and more than half of them show statistical proof that prayer even works at a distance. Dossey says that this is a phenomenal finding and that prayer research is very important in forcing this re-evaluation. He cites the testimony of spiritual healers that empathy, compassion and deep caring are of vital importance in the success of intercessory prayer.

Dr. Dossey says, "Once anyone begins to recognize the infinite wisdom that's contained in prayer, the pressure to 'do it all' eases. A prayer such as 'Thy will be done' suggests that there is an infinite wisdom in the universe that we can access and call upon, and that this wisdom will act through us in benevolent and loving ways. Through prayer, we acknowledge that there's a greater wisdom and a higher power than our own. And through prayer, we get in touch with this higher power so that we can bring miracles into our lives." It is important to note that he does not recommend abandoning medical or surgical treatments and using only prayer, but he does feel that a complementary approach is best—one which uses the best of modern medicine and prayer.

*   *   *   *

A very interesting and informative book on the mind/body connection is *Fire in the Soul, A New Psychology of Spiritual Optimism* by Joan Borysenko, Ph.D. She co-founded and is a former director of the Mind/Body Clinic at New England Deaconess Hospital and was an instructor in medicine at Harvard Medical School. She was one of the architects of psychoneuroimmunology, a cell biologist, and a licensed psychologist.

Joan Borysenko combines her knowledge in the field of psychology with a strong belief in the spiritual side of every person. In her counseling and teaching she emphasizes the necessity of letting go of the past in order to move into the future. She believes we make choices in crisis situations. Borysenko says that if a person believes he is a helpless victim, he is likely to remain anxious, depressed and angry. This attitude and the feelings of loss of control have been linked to decreased immune function and other health problems. Each person is a result of all of his life experiences and the author believes that we need to connect deeply and thankfully with life by loving ourselves, one another and God.

Borysenko addresses many of the questions we all ask, such as, why do human beings suffer and is there a personal God who punishes us? She takes us on a journey as she searches for meaning and a healthy life. She tells us that she looked for answers in the study of philosophy but feels she learned the most from her own trials and those of friends, family and clients. In other words, we learn by living. If we can get past our anger, fear and depression, each crisis presents us with an opportunity for growth. She says, "Some of the healthiest people I know are those who have had to heal from the most challenging situations and, in the process, have gained insight and wisdom far beyond what a 'comfortable' life would ordinarily provoke."

* * * *

In their book, *Remarkable Recovery: What Extraordinary Healings Tell Us About Getting Well and Staying Well,* authors Caryle Hirshberg and Marc Ian Barasch have done extensive research on unexplained miraculous cures or spontaneous remissions of cancer. Hirshberg is a co-founder of the Remission Project at the Institute of Noetic Sciences and was research director and co-writer for the *Heart of Healing* television series. Barasch is the author of *The Healing Path,* a widely acknowledged classic in the literature of mind/body medicine. He is a contributing editor of the *Psychology Today* magazine and a producer/writer for Turner Broadcasting.

The medical profession has largely ignored miraculous cures or spontaneous remissions of cancer because it did not understand them and could not explain them in medical terms. The authors take a serious look at this phenomenon in an attempt to discover a common thread that occurs in cancer patients who survive against all odds.

In the beginning of the book they say, "There are no medical journals devoted to the study of remarkable recovery, those odd instances when a disease such as terminal cancer vanishes almost exorcismally from the body. There are no medical school courses explaining how, on certain irreproducible occasions, a malignant tumor disappears from a CT-scan like a glitch from a radar screen. Though there are institutions devoted to the study of most major diseases, and nationwide networks that trace epidemiology and the treatment efficacies, there is no national remission registry to track unexplained healings. It is not known how often they occur, in what diseases, and in what kinds of people, much less why."

Hirshberg and Barasch go on to present many cases of unexplained cures and to examine the lives of the survivors. They call this quest a 'medical mystery.' Over the years, most physicians have dismissed such cases as flukes. Since those patients who get well after they have been judged by their doctors as terminal do not lend themselves to statistical studies, their case histories are rarely examined: "if we can discern patterns—any patterns—in people who do significantly better and live longer than their conditions would dictate, then, whether they are simply 'nature's own experiments' or the product of the biopsychosocial equation of their lives, we will find information of critical importance in the treatment of disease."

The authors tell us that stories of remarkable recovery are rarely simple. There seems to be an added dimension in the lives of survivors. It is not always the same for each patient, but one common thread does seem to exist—unwillingness to surrender oneself completely to doctors. Time after time, the unlikely survivors mention such things as the power of positive thinking, not giving up, mind/body connection, support of loved ones, reading books on healing, praying for a way back to life and divine intervention.

In research to write their book, they found that some patients get well in spite of the treatment. The authors tell us that current statistics suggest that with the exception of childhood cancers and certain rare forms of the disease, survival has not improved much over the last twenty years. For four of the most common cancers (colon, rectum, pancreas, and lung) there is, says UCLA internist Martin F. Shapiro, no convincing evidence that chemotherapy offers any benefit whatsoever, though many patients receive the treatment. On the other hand, in the stories of remarkable recoveries, the things people actually do cannot be found in case reports. Some alternative forms of medicine, once seen as quack remedies, placebos, or at best unproved therapies, may become the basis for tomorrow's 'real' medicine.

All kinds of alternative or complementary therapies came up over and over in their interviews with patients. Their doctors were baffled at their survival, but the patients believed that many things contributed to their recovery including lifestyle changes and spiritual renewal.

The work of Candace Pert, research scientist, is discussed elsewhere in this book as proof of an added dimension that some cancer patients seem to have that facilitates their healing. Suffice it to say here that her findings validate what all these authors are trying to tell us about heath and well being.

Hirshberg and Barasch believe that the mind/body connection can no longer be ignored in the treatment of any illness. In their quest to find a common thread in remarkable recoveries, they discovered there were diverse approaches to healing depending on individual personalities. There was a certain quality which they called 'congruence'—an impression that these people, in the midst of crisis, had discovered a way to be deeply true to themselves, manifesting a set of behaviors growing from the roots of their being.

CHAPTER 21

BCG AND THE FDA

Cancer is big business. It is the source of enormous income for research institutions, hospitals, doctors and pharmaceutical companies. It is hardly believable but a fact that our health is determined by the pharmaceutical companies. They decide to a large degree which drugs are funded and promoted. These decisions are seldom altruistic.

An example was Dr. Coley who was never able to ever persuade the scientific community to accept or even test his toxins. His experience shows us how difficult it is to get new treatments to the patient. (Details in Chapter 22). Dr. Coley's problems were not an isolated incidence.

Candace Pert and her husband, Michael Ruff, discovered this when they resigned from the NIH and went to work in the private sector in 1987. The pressure to produce something profitable was enormous. When the investors decided to go with the development of the drug AZT instead of Peptide T, their funding was withdrawn and they and twenty-five staff members were out of a job.

*　　　　*　　　　*　　　　*

In his book, *A Commotion in the Blood*, Stephen Hall tells us about the politics and competition in research and the rush to be the first to publish, often prematurely. He illustrates this with the story of Steven Rosenberg's work with Lak cells and Il-2 in 1985. On the basis of treatment of just a few patients, it was reported as a breakthrough. Hall says, "Like interferon before it, the Rosenberg protocol was about to experience all the hype, all the backlash——all the exaggerations of both optimism and disillusionment——mustered by a society that seizes upon the secular miracles of modern medicine and blows them up into phenomena of monstrous dimensions."

*   *   *   *

I have had personal experience with the drug Bacillus Calmette Guerin (BCG) which illustrates how the FDA and drug companies affect our lives. BCG is a non-toxic vaccine that has been used for many years in the treatment of tuberculosis. For the treatment of cancer, it is still on the FDA Investigational New Drug (IND) list.

I had a radical mastectomy for breast cancer in 1969. At that time, the patient had no choice. You signed a release form before the biopsy was performed and if the biopsy confirmed cancer, the surgery was performed immediately. It seems unbelievable now, but you did not know that you had cancer until waking from the surgical procedure. There were no detectable cancer cells in my lymph nodes and I was pronounced cured. No treatment was recommended. In fact, the surgeon used those famous, (if not necessarily true), words, 'I got it all.' Four years later my cancer had metastasized to the bone. By what I still consider a miracle, my surgeon sent me to Dr. Warner who was the only doctor in this area who would recommend treatment other than radiation and/or chemotherapy.

At that time, I did not know anything about the immunotherapy program he proposed to me as therapy. However, it made sense to me that he wanted to build up my immune system instead of destroying it with toxic drugs. My treatment consisted of BCG by scarification, vitamins and other lifestyle changes such as diet, exercise and spiritual renewal. I received four radiation treatments to the pelvic area. I never had chemotherapy. Everything that was done for me was to help my body heal itself and to enhance the quality of my life. I never had any side effects except a slight temperature for twenty-four hours. I have never had any spread of cancer since 1973. I have lived twenty-eight years of a very productive and happy life and I am positive I would not be alive today if I had opted for any other kind of therapy.

*   *   *   *

My husband, Ben, was diagnosed with bladder cancer in 1974. His urologist recommended chemotherapy. Because of the success of my treatment, he chose to be treated by Warner. BCG by scarification was tried but it did not work. Ben continued to have surface tumors that had to be removed. Warner then injected the BCG directly into the bladder. He used to get his treatments on the way home from work and never had any side effects at all. His cancer was under control for sixteen years when he died of complications of heart problems unrelated to the cancer. The autopsy showed many other problems but no cancer at the time of his death. A research urologist at a local hospital told me that BCG was the most effective treatment for bladder cancer, but they could not use it because of the fact that it was considered an experimental drug. Dr. Warner was able to use BCG because he practiced in a private clinic not dependent on federal funds.

The insurance companies would not pay for this treatment because of its experimental status. I called the FDA in the early years of my husband's treatments and was told BCG would probably never be taken off the IND list because it was an inexpensive drug and no pharmaceutical company would ever ask that it be removed. The FDA did not say that BCG was harmful or ineffective, just that it was not profitable.

On April 24, 1981, I wrote to then FDA Commissioner Arthur Hall Hayes in an effort to get BCG removed from the IND list. Portions of my letter said, "In talking to people at the FDA, I get the distinct impression that there has been little effort to evaluate the effectiveness of BCG. I have been told that the FDA considers the drug harmless, but that there are not sufficient studies to prove that it is beneficial in the treatment of cancer. My own research convinces me that this is not true. There is a great deal of positive information on this subject. I am not suggesting that BCG is a cure all for cancer or that it works for everyone, but then neither do radiation or chemotherapy. In the last twelve years, I have watched dozens of cancer victims die miserable, horrible deaths that were treated with radiation and chemotherapy. Immunotherapy has minimal side effects and allows the cancer patient a quality of life that is not possible with other accepted treatments. In my opinion, there is no valid reason to continue to call the use of BCG alone or in combination with other drugs experimental.

Millions of dollars have been poured into the battle against cancer by the government and the results are shockingly poor. I suggest you read the publication, *Hearings before the Subcommittee on Health and Scientific Research of the Committee on Labor and Human Resources: United States Senate-Ninety Sixth Congress.* From beginning to end, there is very little encouraging news for the cancer patient. And yet so many doctors stubbornly insist on repeating the same old treatments that, in most cases, do not work. I would like to see immunotherapy made more available to those who want it.

*   *   *   *

On July 23, 1981, I received the following reply from Harry M. Meyer, Jr., M.D., Director, Bureau of Biologics, Department of Health and Human Services.

"Your letter of April 24, 1981, addressed to Commissioner Hayes was referred to the Bureau of Biologics, Food and Drug Administration (FDA) since our Bureau is responsible for FDA's regulation of biological products such as BCG vaccine.

"We can appreciate your interest in BCG vaccine and its use in the treatment of patients with cancer since all would agree that present methods of treating most forms of cancer are far from ideal. Furthermore, BCG vaccine is one of a group of products referred to as 'biological response modifiers' and the evaluation of modifiers is receiving much attention in cancer research.

"Let me assure you that our scientific staff is familiar with this area of work. Our Bureau is located at the National Institutes of Health campus and our scientists have a great deal of professional contact with the National Cancer Institute and other groups involved in the evaluation of biological response modifiers. Members of our Bureau attended the international conference that you mentioned as well as other pertinent scientific meetings.

"BCG vaccine was licensed by our Bureau many years ago and since that time has been generally available to physicians. Thus, the matter you mentioned relates to recommendations for routine use rather than availability. Manufacturers of biologicals distribute a package circular with their products to guide physicians. The manufacturer's recommendations for use must be approved by our Bureau. Manufacturers would normally propose a new use when in their assessment there was agreement in the scientific community at large that the information available supported the new use. At present the package circulars accompanying commercially distributed BCG vaccine speak to its administration in the prevention of tuberculosis since there is international scientific agreement that the product is safe and effective for this use in the dosage recommended. No manufacturer has proposed to include a recommendation that BCG vaccine be used routinely in the treatment of cancer. Thus, our Bureau has in no way delayed consideration of the matter; rather, manufacturers and experts in the field of cancer therapy are seeking more data as the basis for scientific recommendation."

*   *   *   *

Nothing has changed since 1981 except the approval of BCG as a treatment for bladder cancer because of the efforts of hundreds of urologists. In 1989, 1600 urologists petitioned the FDA for rapid approval of BCG as a treatment for bladder cancer. In an article in *Physicians'*

Weekly on July 17, 1989, West Virginia urology chief Donald Lamm told the American Society of Clinical Oncology that BCG clearly out-performs doxorubicin (Adriamycin, Adria) and is much cheaper.

The article went on to say, "BCG is approved only for TB. Medicare and many other insurance carriers will not pay for it for bladder can-cer. But a doxorubicin regimen is 3.5 times as expensive", Dr. Lamm adds, "and mitomycin—also in trial vs. BCG costs five times as much"….Dr. Lamm gave four-year results of a 285 patient random-ized Southwest Oncology Group study. It showed BCG far better than doxorubicin for both Ta and T1 transitional-cell carcinoma and for car-cinoma in situ, with similar toxicity.

"Among transitional-cell patients, recurrence was 78% after 11 months with doxorubicin, vs. 61% after 22 months with BCG. Of patients with in situ disease, 74% had a complete response to BCG, vs. 42% for doxorubicin. Some 15% taking BCG had progression, vs. 37%

"Time to treatment failure averaged under six months for doxoru-bicin but more than four years for BCG."

The FDA did approve BCG for this specific use. In all probability, my husband was one of the first patients to receive BCG for bladder cancer. It saddens me to think of all the lives it might have saved had it been available to patients many years earlier.

*   *   *   *

I am familiar with other patients who received BCG. One was a Stage IV ovarian cancer patient who was given two months to live by her doctors. They recommended chemotherapy but didn't say it would save her life. That was twenty years ago and she is still alive and well. There was a breast cancer patient with eighteen cancerous lymph nodes out of twenty-eight. Her primary treatment was BCG and she has never had any metastasis of her cancer. Another was a melanoma patient who had only BCG and lived. I know of many more too numerous to mention here.

I wrote to Michael A. Friedman, FDA Commissioner, on August 25, 1997 asking again what steps needed to be taken to remove BCG, a harmless vaccine which boosts the immune system, from the IND list. I asked these questions, "Why, when your agency approves so many harmful, toxic drugs, can you not make available a vaccine with potential benefits to thousands of cancer patients?" And, "if BCG is now considered safe and effective as a therapy for bladder cancer, why wouldn't it be just as effective for other cancers?"

*   *   *   *

Ron Varsaci, Policy Analyst, FDA Executive Secretariat, responded to my letter to Friedman on September 8, 1997. I quote it in its entirety.

"This is in response to your August 25, 1997, letter to Dr. Michael A. Friedman, Lead Deputy Commissioner of the Food and Drug Administration (FDA), requesting information on how BCG vaccine can be approved for the treatment of all cancers. Please let me begin this response by noting that Dr. Friedman (in his last position, he worked in cancer research) is deeply interested in this Agency's stewardship of any improvement in the treatment of cancer. This Agency is committed to reviewing, and, when appropriate, approving new drug applications in the shortest possible time.

"There is no single route to the approval of a new drug. In some cases, a pharmaceutical company may target a specific disease or medical condition. In others, company scientists may independently pursue a promising line of research. In still other situations, a pharmaceutical company may follow-up work begun by researchers from universities, government, or private institutions. However, in all cases, a sponsor must file a new drug application for review by this Agency. (Within the Agency, the developer/manufacturer is commonly referred to as 'the sponsor').

"The Federal Food, Drug, and Cosmetic Act (FFD&C Act) requires FDA to ensure that new drugs are safe and effective. Under the law, FDA reviews the results (scientific data) of studies conducted and submitted by the sponsor of the drug. The purpose of this review is to determine if the drug is safe and effective, to determine whether the drug can be safely sold to the public, and to determine what the new drug's labeling should say about directions for use, side effects, and warnings. The FFD&C Act does not place the responsibility to develop new drugs on the Agency.

"You are correct in your understanding that BCG vaccine has already received FDA approval for treating bladder cancer. As an approved product, BCG vaccine is currently available by prescription. Once a drug is approved for a specific use, physicians may prescribe that drug for other uses they deem appropriate, with the understanding that not all cancers will necessarily respond the same way to a particular medication. This Agency has been concerned that this practice, the off-label use of prescription drugs, has discouraged many drug companies from conducting the necessary studies that would result in a 'supplemental indication' or new drug use being added to the drug label. FDA recently proposed a 'New Use' initiative to encourage pharmaceutical manufacturers to speed up the development and approval of supplemental indications. Under this initiative, FDA has proposed draft guidance describing the quantity and quality of evidence for establishing the safety and effectiveness of new, unlabeled uses of approved drugs. We hope that this guidance will encourage drug manufacturers to apply for and obtain approved labeling and thereby reduce the level of, and the need for, off-label prescriptions. This draft guidance entitled, 'FDA Approval of New Cancer Treatment Uses for Marketed Drug and Biological Products', (copy enclosed), is intended to clarify the evidence that would be sufficient for Agency approval of supplemental cancer treatments.

"In summary, we appreciate your interest in new treatments for cancer. However, a sponsor must be willing to conduct the necessary clinical studies to show that a new treatment is both safe and effective for its indicated use. Therefore, we suggest that you contact one of the current manufacturers of BCG vaccine to investigate their interest in pursuing these approvals."

The lengthy draft guidance they sent me supported previous correspondence that if a pharmaceutical company asked to have BCG approved for use in cancer treatment, it would be seriously considered. Although it is not illegal to use it, the treatment (except for bladder cancer) is still not covered by medical insurance.

*   *   *   *

An interesting sidelight to all this are remarks made by Steven Rosenberg in his book, *The Transformed Cell*, about the use of BCG. Rosenberg is a nationally recognized researcher in the field of immunology.

In his book, Rosenberg makes statements about the effectiveness of BCG I find hard to believe because of my own experience and others under Warner's care. Commenting on a study using BCG for patients with melanoma and bone cancer he says, "This protocol subsequently demonstrated that BCG had no effect on the cancers, but it could put patients through new agonies." Again he says…. "in 1976, both our clinical and lab work in immunotherapy was disappointing. The randomized protocols with BCG were demonstrating its ineffectiveness, and the complications and pain BCG caused our patients made it worse than futile."

I thought his conclusions were amazing so I wrote to him in April 1995. I thought it would be possible he would be interested in Warner's success with this drug without the side effects Rosenberg wrote about. It seemed to me that it would be valuable to his research to know about actual patients who survived and why. With Warner's permission, I suggested Rosenberg contact him. He never did contact Warner nor answer my letter and that has always puzzled me. Why wouldn't he want to know how Warner was using this drug to obtain such different results?

All of which reminds me of a statement made to me many times by Warner. He said, "Since we don't have a cure for cancer, wouldn't it be beneficial if we could all work together, sharing information——our successes and our failures."

*   *   *   *

I present this information and correspondence with the FDA to verify that it has never been illegal to use BCG in the treatment of cancer. So those charges by some of the doctors at the Tumor Institute were entirely fabricated.

When I was a patient at the Tumor Institute of Swedish Hospital, I knew that they were the leaders in Seattle in the investigation and application of immunological therapies. The University of Washington has been conducting research in immunology for years, but they did not then or now treat patients with this promising modality. Why the Tumor Institute would abandon this approach without further investigation has always been a mystery to me.

CHAPTER 22

FURTHER RESEARCH AND DEVELOPMENTS

Since the late 1890s and early 1900s when Coley discovered that stimulating the immune system contributed to recovery from cancer, there have been many hopeful discoveries in this field. Each of these discoveries has been hyped by the news media as a possible cure and the competition amongst research scientists for recognition and research money has been intense. Interferon is an example. Its discovery in 1956 is credited to a Swiss biologist, Jean Lindenmann, and to Alick Isaacs while they were working together at the National Institute for Medical Research in England (Mill Hill) on a series of experiments on viral interference. Interferon turned out to be one of the many responses of the body's immune system to infection by viruses. It is a molecule made by cells that would later become known as part of the family of molecules known as cytokines. It was one thing to discover interferon, but it could only be produced in small amounts at great cost. So the race was on, especially by pharmaceutical companies, to find a way to mass produce it and make it available to the consumer at a reasonable price because of the prospect of huge profits.

Nature produces interferon in infinitesimal quantities, but recombinant DNA could produce it in bulk. There are three kinds of interferon:

alpha, beta and gamma. At the time, all the efforts were focused on producing alpha-interferon, which was being hailed as a miracle cure for everything from cancer to the common cold. Unfortunately, the original claims could not be substantiated although interferon has been useful in combination with other therapies.

Steven Rosenberg is a surgeon and researcher for the National Cancer Institute (NCI). He has been involved in immunotherapy research since 1968. In addition to his research into the interferons, he has investigated BCG, interleukins, tumor necrosis factor, LAK cells (lymphokine-activated killer cells) and IL-2, gene therapy and many others. He has had some successes and many failures. Thirty years of research and still no practical application for patients, which is definitely discouraging for the person diagnosed with cancer.

Rosenberg had experienced 75 straight clinical failures without even a partial success when he began an aggressive protocol using LAK cells and high-dose interleukin-2 (IL-2). His first patients had dangerous, life-threatening side effects, but after some success with a few patients the news was out. The cover of the November 25, 1985 New England Journal of Medicine headlined this latest experimental treatment as 'CANCER BREAKTHROUGH'

Rosenberg became an instant celebrity appearing on television, featured on magazine covers and even received a $100,000 Armand Hammer Cancer Prize in 1985. He later commented that the media hype got totally out-of-hand and raised expectations to incredibly unrealistic levels. When the media latches on to a new, experimental treatment, they often fail to mention long hospitalization, devastating side effects and astronomical costs.

Stephen Hall, in his book *Commotion in the Blood*, is critical of Rosenberg and says he actually courts the spotlight. Also, he apparently has aroused considerable resentment amongst his colleagues for not sufficiently crediting the work of others.

Later the use of LAK cells and IL-2 together or IL-2 alone came under severe criticism from different sources. One of these critics was Charles G. Moertel, oncologist at the Mayo Clinic, saying, "IL-2 therapy as administered in these studies is associated with unacceptably severe toxicity and astronomical costs. These are not balanced by any persuasive evidence of true net therapeutic gain. This specific treatment approach would not seem to merit further application in the compassionate management of patients with cancer."

After the initial publicity, grants of large amounts of money were given to six institutions and no one, including Rosenberg, has reported data comparable to Rosenberg's initial results. The use of LAK cells has been abandoned entirely although there are ongoing studies in the application of IL-2.

*   *   *   *

Another instance of hopeful research involved the use of antibodies. In 1984, Grant Fjermedal, a former writer for the Associated Press specializing in science and medicine, published a book, *Magic Bullets*, in which he explains the use of polyclonal and monoclonal antibodies as the newest technique in the fight against cancer. He calls these antibodies 'magic bullets' because there was much hope at that time that they would seek out and destroy cancer cells while ignoring normal cells.

Fjermedal writes about the limitations of radiation and chemotherapy that we all know so well. In the author's opinion, with the exception of some rare types of cancer, chemotherapy by itself often does not offer much more than agony and false hope. If surgery, radiation or chemotherapy leave a single cancer cell behind, the disease will reestablish itself.

So with cancers that become metastatic, surgery is ineffective, radiation is limited, and chemotherapy usually is nonproductive. What has always been so desperately needed has been a way to go after cancer on a cell-by-cell basis, to unleash the hounds, to find the 'magic bullets'.

Fjermedal spent weeks with Dr. Stanley Order at the Johns Hopkins Oncology Center observing his work with cancer patients. Order was working with polyclonal antibodies involving mostly patients with liver cancer, or hepatoma, and he had achieved remission in 52 percent of his cases. All of the patients admitted to the study were inoperable and considered terminal. So, of course, this seemed very hopeful.

These observations were made 14 years ago. Again, the claims for a miracle cure were premature. How are antibodies being used today and with what success? After more than two decades of disappointing research with monoclonal antibodies at Stanford University, it appears that they have finally proven of limited worth against certain cancers.

*   *   *   *

It is unfortunate that there have been premature hype and expectations for new cancer drugs. What happened with monoclonal antibodies may be happening again with gene therapy. Interleukin-12 has not lived up to original promises. Still, research laboratories all over the world are involved in efforts to find a better way to treat cancer. Many, including Rosenberg's laboratory, are in a race to develop cancer vaccines. The first T-cell-specific antigens have been discovered in Brussels and early tests of a cancer vaccine based on those antigens have been promising in Frankfurt. In Seattle, the adoptive transfer of cloned T cells has been shown to protect immunodeficient patients against disease. In Lausanne, scientists have developed a combination of surgery and cytokine therapy that is saving both lives and limbs. And there are many more labs around the world that are devoting their energies and resources to the seemingly insoluble task of finding a cure for cancer.

Recent medical history abounds with stories of cancer 'cures' that produced exciting results in animals and later proved disappointing when applied to humans. Dr. Richard Klausner, director of the National Cancer Institute recently said, "The history of cancer research has been a history of curing cancer in the mouse. We have cured mice of cancer or decades—and it simply didn't work in humans."

*   *   *   *

Taxol is still another example of a highly touted drug that has not lived up to the original hype. The first problem was the cost and the problem of supply as taxol is produced from the bark of the yew tree. The FDA approved the drug in 1992 for the treatment of advanced ovarian cancer, and in 1994 for advanced breast cancer that has not responded to other medicines. It is given by intravenous infusion in a doctor's office. Seldom mentioned are the devastating side effects, often more debilitating than chemotherapy and most often the cause of a dangerous decline in the number of immune-system cells. Recent articles have suggested that clinical trials prove that taxol can be effective if given in the earlier stages of disease.

The latest study was the first to focus on women with an early stage of breast cancer, in which tumor cells have spread to the lymph nodes but no farther. All of the women were treated with surgery followed by doxorubican and cyclophosphmide, today's most potent breast cancer drug combination. Some women in the study also received infusions of taxol every three weeks for twelve weeks. Patients in the trials have been followed for four years and claims are made that those receiving taxol in addition to other chemotherapy drugs have a longer survival rate. Little is mentioned about the side effects. As is so often the case, the treatment seems worse than the disease.

Tamoxifen is still another drug that has great possibilities to lessen the potential for recurrence of cancer in patients with breast or ovarian cancer. While estrogen is a growth stimulator, tamoxifen is an estrogen inhibitor. It reacts with the estrogen receptor on the surface of estrogen receptor cells.

It is usually given after the cancer has manifested itself. However, there are ongoing protocols to study the benefits for high-risk patients to begin taking tamoxifen before any disease is advanced enough to be diagnosed.

Some patients have reported side effects of hot flashes and there are some reports of endometrial (uterus) cancer after taking Tamoxifen. For this reason, any patient should be carefully watched with regular examinations so if this occurs it can be treated early. Most scientific evidence seems to support that the benefits far outweigh the risks.

*   *   *   *

The latest 'miracle cure' to hit the media via television, magazines and newspapers, following the lead of the New York Times, are the new drugs angiostatin and endostatin. Unlike traditional chemotherapeutic agents, the drugs attack the tumor's blood supply—not the tumor itself—cutting off the tumor's source of nourishment.

Dr. Judah Folkman, a cancer researcher at Children's Hospital in Boston, discovered the drugs *25 years ago*. Folkman's theory was that drugs that blocked the production of angiogenesis factors might prevent tumors from growing larger. It took him all these years to convince the medical community that there was some merit to his theory. Now more than 100 academic laboratories and 40 biotechnology companies are in the race to develop these drugs. In spite of the many years that Dr. Folkman has been investigating this approach, the media would have us believe that angiostatin and endostatin have just suddenly burst upon the scene.

This is a great disservice to those who have cancer and are desperate for something that will save their lives. They flood their doctor's offices with frantic calls when any widespread application of these drugs is years away if at all. There have been limited human trials and those have not been very promising. There are still many obstacles: producing enough of the two 'miracle' proteins to test in humans, who will get the drugs first, at what price, and will they be covered by insurance. The testing protocol required by the FDA includes two more years of tests in animals to prove the drugs are not dangerously toxic, then, finally, clinical trials in humans. What never appears in the headlines is that it will probably be years before all the questions are resolved.

*   *   *   *

This discussion of cancer treatments would not be complete without examining the benefits and disadvantages of bone marrow transplants. Here in Seattle, the Fred Hutchinson Cancer Research Center (FHCRC) is world renowned for this procedure. The treatment itself is described by patients as so agonizing and painful it is beyond description. Before the transplant, powerful drugs are administered in order to completely knock out the immune system, which brings the patient to death's door. If this initial phase is survived, the transplant is performed and the patient must take immune suppressant drugs the rest of his life to prevent rejection. A recent patient, Carl Sagan, the famed astronomer, was treated with a bone marrow transplant at FHCRC. He did not die of cancer—he died of pneumonia.

Anyone who is contemplating this procedure should call the CANCER HOTLINE and ask for the National Institutes of Health publication, *Bone Marrow Transplantation and Peripheral Blood Cell Transplantation*. This report discusses in readable detail what a patient needs to know before submitting to this course of action in the management of his disease. It explains the procedure, the side effects and the costs. Transplantation of bone marrow or peripheral blood stem cells involves potentially serious risks, and patients require the care of skilled medical staff and support services. Many patients and their families have to move far from home for many months for in-patient and outpatient treatments, which adds to already horrendous costs. This treatment is denied to patients who are not covered by insurance or cannot raise the funds to pay for it upfront.

This publication's discussion of the side effects is particularly chilling. It tells us that many patients need a full year to recover physically and psychologically from transplantation. Even after that period, life may not return to 'normal', the way it was before the illness. Medication may be necessary indefinitely, and the patient's lifestyle may have to be changed to help prevent fatigue, avoid infectious diseases, and cope with the long-term effects of treatment.

The NIH lists the physical changes as dry eyes, skin sensitivity, reproductive disorders (infertility), liver function, gastrointestinal problems, high blood pressure, and, in some cases, seizures and problems with vision. Temporary side effects also may produce bone pain, muscle aches, and flu-like symptoms. Life-threatening infections include a type of fungus (Aspergillus) and pneumonia. Less troubling but serious are shingles, cold sores, genital herpes, and inflammation of the mouth and gastrointestinal tract. In an attempt to counteract these infections, antiviral agents, antibiotics, and antifungal agents are given before and after the transplant.

Graft-Versus-Host Disease (GVHD) is one of the most serious potential complications of bone marrow transplant. It occurs when T cells in the donated marrow (the graft) identify the recipient's body (the host) as foreign and attack it. Common symptoms of acute GVHD are skin rashes, jaundice, liver disease, and diarrhea. Because recovery of immune function after BMT, (bone marrow transplant) is delayed, patients also have persistent susceptibility to infections. Patients with mild forms of acute GVHD are likely to recover completely, but those with severe forms may die of complications. Chemotherapy, radiation therapy, antibiotics, and immunosuppressive agents (especially cyclosporine) also may cause kidney failure. Every organ in the body, including the lungs and the heart, are susceptible to serious damage. I have attempted to get statistics on the survival rate of this extreme treatment but I am always told that there are none available. I am sure there are statistics available but apparently not to the general public. They could be obtained under the Freedom of Information Act.

CHAPTER 23

IMMUNOLOGY, RADIATION & CHEMOTHERAPY

What progress has been made in the treatment of cancer in the last 50 to 100 years? Certainly we know that in the 1900s not much was offered in the way of treatment except surgery and that was crude at best. Amazingly enough, a Dr. William B. Coley stumbled onto an immune response in a few patients in the late 1800s. He was already well known and respected in surgical circles when surgical intervention was the only recourse for cancer patients.

To simplify a very complicated and life-long quest, one of Dr. Coley's terminal patients, after repeated surgeries and recurrence of his cancer, developed a high fever diagnosed as erysipelas. To the amazement of Coley and all of the hospital staff, this man's tumors disappeared and he remained disease free for many years. This incident led Coley to examine literature and medical cases of what were called 'spontaneous remissions' and his was undoubtedly the first serious venture into immunology. There were others before him going back to the 1700s who observed favorable outcomes in cancer cases that were often accompanied by infection. Some physicians even tried bizarre infection-induced treatments.

However, Coley was the first to develop a toxin that he used on terminally ill patients over a period of many years. Today, he would be accused of malpractice for subjecting a patient to a treatment that had not been clinically tested. On May 3, 1891, Coley infected a patient with cultures of erysipelas and in the process started the American era of cancer immunology. Even though, at that time, he had no understanding of how the immune system worked, he recognized that an infection somehow stimulated the body to affect the tumor. It would be many years later before scientists would discover the complicated mechanisms involved in provoking an immune response in the body.

It took five attempts with ever-increasing dosage of the erysipelas cultures before this first patient elicited a response, but eventually the patient responded in a miraculous way. His tumor diminished in size and his general condition was good when, prior to the injection, he was not expected to live. He lived for another eight and a half years. Further successful cases followed, but there were some failures, too, because of the potency of the cultures. The injection of erysipelas and resulting high fever did reduce the size of the tumors, but also, in some instances, killed the patient.

The successes Coley did have started him on a quest for a toxin (or therapeutic vaccine) and eventually led him to abandon the use of live bacteria. He reported many successes, but other doctors were not able to duplicate his results. This was largely due to the fact that he never developed a quality controlled product. There was no standardized formulation, a standard form of administration or a recommended amount of time for the duration of the treatment.

The controversy over the use of Coley toxins raged for many years and one of the main antagonists was James Ewing who would become Coley's boss. Ewing became a strong advocate of radiation therapy as a cure-all for cancer. Originally, a colleague and supporter of Coley toxins, by 1912 he had become extremely negative. In a paper he published at that time titled, *The Treatment of Cancer on Biological Principles*, he did not mention a single instance of Coley's work. This omission came in spite of the fact that Coley claimed close to 200 durable cures at that time.

The debate continued for many years and in a symposium in 1934, Coley presented his results and asked for fair clinical trials to test the efficacy of his toxins. A surprising ally at that time was a surgeon named Ernest A. Codman who had worked with Coley in the 1920s. At that time, along with Ewing and Joseph Colt Bloodgood, a surgeon at Johns Hopkins Medical School, Codman attempted to completely discredit the Coley toxins. Yet this same Codman, in 1934, had made a complete reversal of his professional judgment. His words were recorded in the American Journal of Surgery.

"It seems to me beyond a doubt that he (Coley) has convincing evidence to show that the mixed toxins are of value in the treatment of sarcoma, and especially in the type now called Ewing's sarcoma. Just as it has seemed quite justifiable for the Memorial Hospital during the last decade to test out the value of radiation alone in inoperable cases or in patients opposed to operation, so it seems indicated that some great clinic should try out Coley's toxins during the next decade. Unquestionably, they produce a profound constitutional effect, and their administration is followed by a marked increase in the production of lymphocytes. It may be that the activity of the lymphocytes accounts for the occasional miracle, which follows this treatment. It is time for some great hospital to apply its laboratory resources to the wholly justifiable and distinctly hopeful purpose of giving this treatment a fair trial under favorable conditions."

No such trial was ever conducted and perhaps a great opportunity for understanding the role of the immune system in the treatments of cancer was lost for many years.

*   *   *   *

By coincidence, the last two known survivors treated with Coley toxins live in a retirement home ten minutes from where I live on Mercer Island just outside of Seattle, Washington. One of them is Dr.

William L. Curtis, 86 years old, and the other is Eric Hanson, 99 years old, who lives at Mercer Island Covenant Shores with his 90 year old wife. Both of these men attribute their survival to the Coley toxins.

On November 18, 1997, Helen and Glenn Warner and I had the privilege of having dinner with Dr. Curtis and a two hour conversation about his cancer experience. It was in 1921 when he was 12 years old that Curtis was diagnosed with an osteogenic sarcoma of the femur (bone cancer).

Six months before the diagnosis of cancer, he had scarlet fever and was in bed for eight weeks. After that, he sustained an injury to his leg while working in the basement of his home and was taken to a doctor because of considerable pain. The doctor thought he had a hemorrhage under the skin, but after x-rays and a biopsy confirmed a tumor he started radiation treatments. This had no effect on the tumor at all. Then radiation implants were tried: the doctor put the needles into his leg in the morning and took them out at night.

The accepted treatment then for this type of cancer was amputation of his leg which his father rejected in the initial stages. He and his family lived in the Seattle area, but after extensive research, were able to obtain the Coley toxins which were administered once a week. The side effects were chills and a fever of 104 to 105 degrees overnight. Six months after the treatments, on the advice of his doctor, his leg was amputated. In later years, Dr. Curtis believed the amputation was not necessary. However, he still believes that the Coley vaccines saved his life.

Dr. Curtis told us that he was the last surviving member of a group of 175 cases collected by Dr. Coley's daughter, Helen Nauts, and her Cancer Research Institute in New York. His case was one of those reported when he was 18 years old and he had survived five years at that time. He feels today that the Coley toxins were a major factor in his survival and the fact that he had no metastasis.

Curtis went on to become a doctor in General Practice and went to work in the Grays Harbor, Hoquiam, Washington area in 1937. He worked very hard during the World War II years because there was such a shortage of civilian doctors. Along with the rest of his medical practice, he told us that he delivered over 1,000 babies.

Eventually, he had a radiology clinic in the North End of Seattle and serviced a series of clinics in the area. He had finished his training in radiation therapy in 1955 at Swedish Hospital Medical Center. During our conversation, Curtis told us that he used to attend Tumor Board meetings at Harborview Hospital in Seattle to speak against amputation, but no one listened to him. He feels that one of the most hopeful things today is the number of people who are turning to alternative medicine.

When Dr. Curtis learned of Warner's difficulties with the State Medical Commission through an article I wrote for a local paper, he wrote him a letter telling of his experience. He closed his letter by writing, "I was unpleasantly surprised to hear that you have suffered severe criticism from local physicians for working with immunotherapy. Dr. Coley suffered similar criticism for his work nearly 100 years ago and the whole idea was smothered by surgeons and re-appeared only recently and is being pushed by the Cancer Research Institute."

Eric Hanson developed bone cancer when he was 18 years old and was treated with Coley toxins. He tells of being drafted by the armed services in 1917 for World War I. When the doctor examining him found he had had an operation to remove tumors and read his doctor's letter he said, "We can't use this fellow because he'll be dead in three months." Hanson told Dr. Coley about this remark and Coley said, "We'll see about that" and he continued his treatment for a year. Both Eric and his wife, Lydia, give extra credit for their longevity to a healthy diet, exercise, vitamins and a strong spiritual life.

*   *   *   *

Part of the problem faced by Coley in advancing his theories was the discovery of a previously unknown form of radiation by Wilhelm Roentgen. He called it x-ray and it burst upon the medical scene as a miracle. It was embraced by the scientific community and the public as the "miracle cure" for cancer. Such enthusiasm would later be proven to be entirely unwarranted. It seems unbelievable today that the medical community would naively accept and use this new method without any scientific studies as to its safety. In the beginning, it was treated as a highly beneficial and harmless way of treating cancer. There was no concern then that x-ray could harm tissue and damage the skin. In fact, it was embraced with reckless abandon as a harmless healing agent.

It was in 1896 that this previously unknown form of radiation was discovered and it was not until 1932 that its use was regulated by the Food and Drug Administration (FDA). In the interim, physicians used it indiscriminately with no controls on dosage or duration of treatment. Of course today it is accepted that radiation in the treatment of cancer has limited success and is certainly not a miracle cure. In fact, in a recent article released by the Associated Press author Emma Ross cites a 30 year study by an international team of researchers. This study says that lung cancer patients treated with radiation after surgery are 20 percent more likely to die than those undergoing only the surgery. The detrimental effect was greatest in patients in the early stages of the disease, the study said. In those with more advanced but still operable lung cancer, the radiation therapy did not seem to cause harm, although it also did not appear to help.

Ross quotes Dr. Gordon McVie, director at the Cancer Research Campaign in London and a lung cancer specialist who was not part of the study as saying, "It (the study) should be compulsory reading for chief executives of hospitals. In many places, this is routine treatment. It has been assumed that it was a good idea. I was unsurprised that radiotherapy didn't prolong survival, but what I'm really concerned about is that it could actually do harm. There is a very clear message here. My question would be, if it didn't prolong survival, why was it being used at all?"

In 1943, a physician named Cornelius P. Rhoads became director of Memorial Sloan-Kettering Cancer Center in New York. During World War II, he headed the medical division of the Army's Chemical

Warfare Division. In this capacity, he became familiar with the chemical agents that made up poisonous mustard gases and would eventually be used in the treatment of cancer and become known as chemotherapy. This was called a great development and pushed the Coley vaccines further into the background of medical science.

Chemotherapy is called a non-specific agent. In other words, it does not specifically target the cancer but healthy tissue as well. Side effects are often devastating symptoms such as nausea, hair loss and suppression of the immune system. Statistics show limited success with both radiation and chemotherapy. Why then are doctors so resistant to the use of other healing modalities including immunotherapy and lifestyle changes?

CHAPTER 24

CONCLUSIONS

I cannot conclude this book without emphasizing again the powerful effect of the mind on the body. Research is proving that positive thinking does strengthen the immune system and promote health.

There are now so many books on the mind/body connection it causes one to wonder if the 'mainstream' doctor is reading or listening. One of the important aspects of all this literature for the reader is the realization that we can make changes before we become ill. It's called prevention—taking care of ourselves physically and emotionally.

I know from my experience that what these authors are trying to tell us is true. If we want to be well, we have to confront the stresses in our lives and work hard to maintain physical and emotional balance.

In my journey to wellness, I have found that reading the literature on the mind/body connection strengthens my determination to stay the course. Deepak Chopra, M.D., writes in *Ageless Body, Timeless Mind* that "We are the only creatures on earth who can change our biology by what we think and feel....Our cells are constantly eavesdropping on our thoughts and being changed by them. A bout of depression can wreak havoc with the immune system; feeling in love can boost it. Despair and hopelessness raise the risk of heart attack and cancer, thereby shortening life. Joy and fulfillment keep us healthy and extend life." Central to the entire theme of this book is the message that we need to love and be loved. There are all kinds of love encompassing the romantic, parent for child, child for parent, for friends, for humanity and, perhaps, the most important of all, the unselfish love to all that expects nothing in return.

*　　　　*　　　　*　　　　*

Dr. Dean Ornish, a highly respected cardiologist, has become well known because of his advocacy of diet and exercise for his heart patients. Now, he has come a step further with his new book *Love and Survival*. In working with patients, he has found that strong social connections to family, friends, community and religion may be even more powerful than traditional medicine in keeping us well. Ornish says, "If you're trained to use drugs and surgery, and not talk to patients, that's what you do. What I'm trying to do is create a new model for medicine that's more caring and compassionate."

This belief is reinforced by such people as Andrew Weil, a Harvard trained physician. He believes that, although traditional medicine is helpful, alternative methods should not be discounted. He would like to see an integration of these seemingly different worlds.

I would recommend reading *The Heart of Healing* by the Institute of Noetic Sciences with William Poole, *The Power Within—True Stories of Exceptional Cancer Patients Who Fought Back With Hope* by Wendy Williams, *Superimmunity: Master Your Emotions and Improve Your Health* by Paul Pearsall, Ph.D. and *Healing the Mind* by Bill Moyers. All of these books, as the others I have referred to, tell us that we need to take charge of our lives. We can affect our health and well being as we move forward with hope.

*　　　　*　　　　*　　　　*

With scientific advances, many of them of great benefit to patients, the human element seems to have been lost along the way. Instead of treating the whole person, the patient is shuffled around from one specialist to another and each of them zero in on their particular area of expertise.

It would seem to be self-evident that to be successful it is necessary to treat more than the cancer. The patients need to be helped in many ways to become healthy in body and mind. Why do so many doctors resist this approach? In fact, there are many who become angry and insist there is no correlation between lifestyle changes and surviving cancer. Could it be because it takes more of the doctor's time to relate to his patients this way? Or is the doctor reluctant to become emotionally involved with his patients?

*   *   *   *

Dr. Bernard Lown's book, *The Lost Art of Healing,* should be required reading for all doctors. He speaks of the importance of the doctor/patient relationship as a partnership and tells the reader that the art of healing involves much more than diagnostic skills and the ability to mobilize technology.

Dr. Lown is professor emeritus of cardiology at the Harvard School of Public Health and senior physician at Brigham and Women's Hospital in Boston. His experience comes from the treatment of patients with heart problems, but his observations are applicable to the care of all patients whatever their illness.

Dr. Lown does not discount the many wonderful scientific advances in medicine, but he does deplore the fact that technology, in many instances, has replaced the closeness of the patient/doctor relationship. He tells us that medicine in the United States is widely regarded as the best in the world. Hardly a day passes without a major scientific breakthrough. Many formerly fatal diseases are now curable. People are healthier and live longer than ever. Still, patient dissatisfaction with doctors has rarely been more acute. Although physicians are increasingly able to cure disease and prolong life, the American public is suspicious, distrustful of, and even antagonistic to, the profession. Doctors, uneasy, astonished, resentful, and angry, universally acknowledge a crisis in health care. With the focus on colossal medical expenditures, amounting to a trillion dollars annually, most of the numerous solutions involve containing runaway costs. This book reaches a different conclusion about what is ailing our health care system.

"Medicine's profound crisis, I believe, is only partially related to the ballooning costs, for the problem is far deeper than economics. In my view, the basic reason is that medicine has lost its way, if not its soul. An unwritten covenant between doctor and patient, hallowed over several millennia, is being broken."

*   *   *   *

There is a recent book by John Robbins titled *Reclaiming Our Health, Exploding the Medical Myth and Embracing the Source of True Healing.* (Robbins is the award winning author of *Diet for a New America* and has long been an advocate of a healthier life style.) He became acquainted with Warner and included a section of his book on his highly effective treatment and his problems with the medical community.

Robbins notes that Warner exemplifies the ability of a physician to bring patients the best of both orthodox and innovative approaches. He interviewed patients who always spoke of an incredible patient/doctor relationship. They felt that Warner cared about them, gave them hope, and they trusted him with their lives. The author makes the statement that Warner's immunotherapy approach had produced a record of achievement with cancer patients that is quite possibly superior to that attained by any other oncologist in the United States.

Robbins attributes the vendetta against this doctor to jealousy and the fact that he defied the 'conventional wisdom' of the medical community. Often, patients other oncologists had given up on and labeled terminal found their way to Dr. Warner and somehow survived. That was embarrassing! He was a threat to their medical training. Instead of trying to learn about the successful methods he used, some doctors decided he was dangerous. Was he dangerous to the patients or other doctors?

This author likens Warner to other pioneers in the field of medicine, those whose ideas were originally rejected—and years later generally accepted.

*   *   *   *

For those who are interested in all the options for cancer treatment, I would recommend a new book by James S. Gordon, M.D. and Sharon Curtin. The title is *Comprehensive Cancer Care: Integrating Alternative, Complementary, and Conventional Therapies.*

James S. Gordon was the first Chairman of the Advisory Council of the National Institutes of Health's Office of Alternative Medicine. A clinical professor of Psychiatry and Family Medicine at the Georgetown University School of Medicine, he is also the Director of The Center for Mind-Body Medicine in Washington, D.C. and the creator of the Comprehensive Cancer Care Conference.

Sharon Curtin is a patient advocate and expert on aging with a background in nursing and community activism. She is also the author of the New York Times Notable books, *Nobody Ever Died of Old Age.*

This is the best book I have read on the resources available to the cancer patient. As I read it, I realized that it contained so much of what Glenn Warner believed, he could have written it. In the introduction, Dr. Gordon says, "In this book we offer you the possibility of living life with cancer in a new, expanded, and joyful way, and of making choices that may significantly prolong your life as well as enhance its quality."

The authors take the reader through the whole cancer experience from the shock of diagnosis to choosing a medical team and treatment. There are chapters on the immune system, mind/body connection, healing connections such as support groups and spiritual renewal, diet and nutrition, Chinese medicine and other alternative choices.

We need to be educated and feel empowered by the fact that we are making choices that are right for us. I feel, and these authors also emphasize, that it is essential that we believe in the course of action *we choose* from all the options presented to us. Hopefully, after the initial shock of being diagnosed with cancer, we can find a way of "looking at the difficulties we face as challenges from which we can grow, rather than as disasters that will inevitably overwhelm us."

I found much hope in this book, hope that the medical community is finally taking seriously what Glenn Warner believed for years: that it is not enough to treat just the disease; that the physician must treat the whole person.

With all of the evidence emerging supporting the concept of treating the whole person and not just the disease, it is time for the medical community to wake up and pay attention.

At the present time, there are dozens of books by reputable scientific professionals that discuss the benefits of the mind/body connection. These authors were not always certain why it worked, but there has been mounting evidence over the years that treating the emotional as well as the physical provides better opportunities for success.

*   *   *   *

Now we have a book by Candace Pert, Ph.D., *Molecules of Emotion*, that ties it all together. The author has impeccable credentials in scientific research, and most recently, has been a research professor in the Department of Physiology and Biophysics at Georgetown Medical Center in Washington, D. C.

Candace Pert has come full circle since her beginnings as a scientist. She has proven that our emotions release chemicals in the body that affect our health. She believes in a lifestyle that promotes prevention of disease and also that the individual has great powers to promote wellness both physically and emotionally.

The story of Candace Pert, her professional and personal life, is fascinating. She was a research scientist in a mostly male world struggling for recognition. She admits to being naive in not playing the game. She thought her discoveries would speak for themselves and be readily accepted. She has fought a medical world that still largely refuses to believe that our emotions have anything to do with our health.

Pert was the scientist who discovered the opiate receptor in 1972, a molecule found on the surface of cells in the body and the brain. Although her boss took credit in subsequent published papers, Pert claims that it was she who found the opiate receptor and found a way to measure it which proved its existence. She says, "unless we can measure something, science won't concede it exists, which is why science refuses to deal with such 'nothings' as the emotions, the mind, the soul, or the spirit."

In her book, the author goes on to explain the significance of this breakthrough in science and how it proves beyond a doubt the importance of understanding how our emotions, both positive and negative, contribute to our well being. Years of research by Pert and others followed to find the natural substance in the body that used the receptor, including studies of peptides. Peptides are tiny pieces of protein which consist of a string of amino acids joined together.

It was in 1986 that the author and her husband, Michael Ruff, proved the existence of peptide T, a binding agent for the opiate receptor. They believed they had made an enormous discovery, one with positive implications in the treatment of AIDS. They believed that a synthesized peptide might be used as a potent antiviral therapeutic to prevent the HIV virus from entering the cells. They could not even get their findings published because of their inability to find a scientist to evaluate their paper. It was even rejected by Albert Sabin, creator of the oral polio vaccine, as having no scientific value. Eventually, it was reviewed by Carleton Gajduesh, a Nobel laureate from the NIH and accepted by *Proceedings of the National Academy of Science*, a journal published by the National Academy of Sciences.

The next step was procuring funding for further trials. The author was a research scientist at the NIH at the time of her discovery of the peptide T. Strangely enough, that institution would never give her the support needed for full testing and development. The prevalent thinking in the medical and scientific fields held firmly to the denial of any important connection between mind and body as they pertained to health and disease. She felt her discoveries were self-evident, but her initiation into the AIDS arena was as frustrating as earlier experiences in cancer research.

There was a funding bonanza for AIDS research at that time and scientists were all scrambling for dollars. The NIH decided to go with AZT, a chemotherapeutic drug with side effects that included destroying the immune system and was never considered a cure. But there were big bucks to be made. Pert resigned. Her book tells a compelling story of the years it has taken to get the scientific community to take seriously the benefits of peptide T for AIDS patients and possibly cancer patients. So, for all this time there was a non-toxic drug that might have made a difference between life and death for hundreds of people.

Then we come to the question of whether suppressed anger or other negative emotions can cause cancer. It is a known fact that all of us have small cancerous tumors growing in our bodies all the time. Our immune system is always geared to reject invaders with a natural killer cell whose job it is to attack any tumors and destroy them. Their job is coordinated by various brain and body peptides and their receptors to rid the body of any cancerous growth. Most of the time these cells are very efficient, but what happens if the flow of peptides is disrupted? The author makes the point that if we are to take seriously the link between the body and the mind we need to examine several questions: can we consciously intervene to make sure our natural killer cells keep doing their job?; could being in touch with our emotions facilitate the flow of peptides?; is emotional health important to physical health?; if it is, what is emotional health?

Pert says, "I believe all emotions are healthy because emotions are what unite the mind and the body. Anger, fear, and sadness, the so-called negative emotions, are as healthy as peace, courage, and joy. To repress these emotions and not let them flow freely is to set up a disintegrity in the system, causing it to act at cross-purposes rather than as a unified whole. The stress this creates, which takes the form of blockages and insufficient flow of peptide signals to maintain function at the cellular level, is what sets up the weakened conditions that can lead to disease. All honest emotions are positive emotions."

*   *   *   *

The words of these authors are especially pertinent in any discussion of Warner's practice of medicine. He always believed that it was important to treat the whole person, not just the disease. He cared about each patient, he listened, he patiently explained the options for therapy and the lifestyle changes he felt were necessary, and explained that the process of healing involves a partnership. He believed that the patient who aggressively took charge had a much better chance of becoming well in all aspects of his/her life.

There was an intangible something Warner gave to each patient that is reflected in the many letters written in support of his care. From my own experience, I remember so well the first time I met him. I was in the hospital for a biopsy to confirm that my breast cancer had metastasized to the bone. I was transported in a wheelchair to the Tumor Institute to talk to him about his recommendations for treatment. I waited quite awhile not knowing what to expect. This man walked into the examining room and even his presence was calming. It's hard to explain, but by the time we had finished talking I was absolutely sure I was going to get well. The best I can describe the intangible was a profound feeling of HOPE—that together we were going to be successful.

Warner's approach accounts for the incredible loyalty of patients and their families. Many people have said to me, "I finally found a doctor who cares about me." This man often seemed to be a throwback to the family doctor of earlier times. He even made house calls. Of course, not all of his patients survived their cancer. Many of them came to him after failing so-called conventional treatments and their disease was already widely disseminated. When loved ones died, he comforted the families and attended their funerals. Grateful family members thanked him for the quality of life he was able to give in the remaining time left. I have never known a doctor so dedicated to his patients. He always worked long hours. Never satisfied with the success of accepted cancer treatments, he was always searching for something better.

BIBLIOGRAPHY

A Commotion in the Blood by Stephen Hall: Publisher, Henry Holt & Company, Inc., 115 West 18th Street, New York, N.Y. Copyright 1997.

Ageless Body, Timeless Mind by Deepak Chopra, M.D.: Publisher, Harmony Books, a division of Crown Publishers, Inc., New York, N.Y. Copyright 1993.

American Journal of Surgery, 1934. Paper by Ernest A. Codman, M.D.

Anatomy of an Illness by Norman Cousins: Publisher, W. W. Norton, 500 5th Avenue, New York, N.Y. 10110. Copyright 1979.

Bone Marrow Transplantation and Peripheral Blood Cell Transplantation: Published by the National Institutes of Health; Department of Health and Human Services. 1993.

Fire in the Soul, A New Psychology of Spiritual Optimism by Joan Borysenko, Ph.D. Publisher, Warner Books, Inc., New York, N. Y. Copyright 1993.

From Victim to Victor by Harold H. Benjamin, Ph.D.: Publisher, Dell Publishing, 666 Fifth Avenue, New York, N. Y. 10103. Copyright 1987.

Getting Well Again by O. Carl Simonton, M.D. and Stephanie Matthew: Publisher, J.P. Tarcher, distributed by St. Martins Press, 200 Madison Avenue, New York, N.Y. 10016. Copyright 1978.

Head First, the Biology of Hope by Norman Cousins: Publishers, E.P. Dutton, a division of Penguin Books USA, Inc., 2 Park Avenue, New York, N.Y. 10016. Copyright 1989.

Healing and the Mind by Bill Moyer: Publisher, Doubleday, a division of Bantam Doubleday Dell Publishing Group, Inc., 666 Fifth Avenue, New York, N.Y. 10103. Copyright 1993.

Healing Journey, Restoring Health and Harmony to Body, Mind and Spirit by O. Carl Simonton, M.D. with Reid Henson and Brenda Hampton: Publisher, Bantam Books, Bantam, Doubleday, Dell Publishing Group, Inc. Copyright 1992.

Hellstrom Research Papers: *Progress in Cancer Research & Therapy, Vol. 6, Immunotherapy of Cancer; Present Status of Trials in Man*: Publishers, Raven Press, 1140 Avenue of the Americas, New York, N.Y. 10036. Copyright 1978. Hellstrom & Brown: The *Antigens*, Vol. 5 , pp. 1-82. 1979 Hellstrom & Hellstrom, *CancerRes.* 39.

Lost Art of Healing by Bernard Lown, M.D.: Publisher, Houghton Mifflin Company, 215 Park Avenue South, New York, N.Y. 10003. Copyright 1996.

Love and Survival by Dean Ornish, M.D.: Publishers, HarperCollins, Inc., 10 E. 53rd St., New York, N.Y. 10022.

Love, Medicine and Miracles by Bernie S. Siegel, M.D.: Publisher, Harper & Row, 10 East 53rd Street, New York, N.Y. 10022. Copyright 1986.

Magic Bullets by Grant Fjermedal: Publisher, Macmillan Publishing Co., 866 Third Avenue, New York, N.Y. 10022. Copyright 1984.

Meaning and Medicine and Healing Words: The Power of Prayer and the Practice of Medicine by Larry Dossey, M.D.: Publisher, Daily Word, a Unity Publication, 1901 NW Blue Parkway, Unity Village, MO 64065.

Molecules of Emotion by Candace Pert, Ph.D.: Publisher, Scribner, 1230 Avenue of the Americas, New York, N.Y. 10020. Copyright 1997

Peace, Love and Healing by Bernie S. Siegel, M.D.: Publisher, Harper & Row, 10 East 53rd Street, New York, N.Y. 10022. Copyright 1989.

Reclaiming Our Health, Exploding the Medical Myth and Embracing the Source of True Healing by John Robbins: Publisher, H. J. Kramer, Inc., P. O. Box 1082, Tiburon, CA 94920. Copyright 1996.

Remarkable Recovery: What Extraordinary Healings Tell Us About Getting Well and Staying Well by Caryle Hirshberg and Marc Ian Barasch: Publisher, Riverhead Books, a division of G. P. Putnam's Sons, 200 Madison Avenue, New York, N.Y. 10016. Copyright 1995.

Superimmunity: Master Your Emotions and Improve Your Health by Paul Pearsall, Ph.D.: Publisher, McGraw-Hill Company, New York, St. Louis, San Francisco, Hamburg, Mexico, Toronto. Copyright 1987.

The Heart of Healing by The Institute of Noetic Sciences with William Poole: Publisher, Turner Publishing, Inc., 1050 Techwood Drive, N.W., Atlanta, Georgia 30318. Copyright 1993.

The Immune System—How It Works: Published by National Institutes of Health, U. S. Department of Health and Human Services. NIH Publication No. 96-3229. Revised December 1993. Reprinted April 1996.

The Power Within—True Stories of Exceptional Cancer Patients Who Fought Back With Hope by Wendy Williams: Publisher, Fireside, Simon/Schuster /HarperCollins, New York N.Y. Copyright 1991.

The Treatment of Cancer on Biological Principles by James Ewing, M.D. Published in 1912.

The Transformed Cell by Steven A. Rosenberg, M.D., Ph.D. and John M. Barry: Publisher, G. P. Putnam's Sons, 200 Madison Avenue, New York, N.Y. 10016. Copyright 1992.

Understanding the Immune System. Published by National Institutes of Health; Department of Health and Human Services. NIH Publication No. 93-529. Revised January 1993.

What's Next Once Cancer Is Cured? By Yochi Dreazen for Knight Ridder newspapers.

Comprehensive Cancer Care, Integrating Alternative, Complementary, And Coventional Therapies by James S. Gordon M.D. and Sharon Curtin. Perseus Publishing, a member of Perseus Books Group. Copyright @ 2000 by James S. Gordon M.D. and Sharon Curtin.